INTRODUCING TRADITIONAL BEDFORDSHIRE LACE

Ring cushion (Patterns 7-10) & Locket (Pattern 17), both worked by Anne-Marie Desrousseaux. Handkerchief (Pattern 12), worked by Dorothy Formston. *Rings* by John Cook, Goldsmiths, Bedford. *Photo* Les Goodey.

Introducing
Traditional Bedfordshire Lace
in 20 lessons

BARBARA UNDERWOOD

RUTH BEAN Carlton, Bedford

Published by
RUTH BEAN
Victoria Farmhouse, Carlton, Bedford MK43 7LP
England

© Ruth Bean 1993
All rights reserved
ISBN 0 903585 27 8

Design Alan Bultitude at the September Press, Irchester, Northamptonshire
Photography Photography Department, Cambridge University Library
Printed in Great Britain by Galliard Printers, Great Yarmouth, Norfolk

Cover: Bookmarks, Patterns 2, 4, & 19; Medallion, Pattern 17

To the memory of Vi Bullard
who gave so much encouragement and who will never be forgotten

Contents

Foreword

Bedfordshire lace has many qualities to inspire the modern lace-maker, as well as a fascinating history, and interest in its traditional methods and techniques has grown considerably in recent years. The publication in 1986 of *Bedfordshire Lace Patterns* and in 1988 of *Traditional Bedfordshire Lace*, intended for the experienced lace-maker, fed this interest but generated many requests for a book explaining traditional methods and techniques to beginners. This book is the practical response!

Acknowledgements

I would like to thank all those who have helped in the preparation of this book; friends and students, including Anne-Marie Desrousseaux, Dorothy Formston, Molly Potts, Pat Rowley, Janet Tarbox and Annie Temple, who kindly lent their lace for photography, contributed ideas and gave encouragement; Eunice Arnold and Sandra King for their valuable comments on the manuscript; Bridget Cook for her enhancement of the diagrams, and Les Goodey for the studio photography. Finally my thanks to Ruth Bean who has unstintingly given her time and expertise throughout the production of this work.

Introduction

This book explains and gives instruction in the techniques of Bedfordshire lace made in the traditional manner, which has its roots in the Bucks Point, Maltese and Honiton laces.

It is intended for those with just basic knowledge of bobbin lace techniques who are newcomers to Bedfordshire lace, and the patterns progress in planned stages through the important features.

By working systematically through the patterns, the lace-maker will acquire a real understanding of the lace, and develop an ability to recognise and work the components of more complicated patterns.

The examples used apply traditional techniques to a mix of modern designs and adaptations of old patterns. A few additional patterns without instructions are included to provide further practice and interest as the lace-maker becomes more proficient, and these are shown in the centre colour plate.

At the start of the book threads are shown individually in the diagrams, but after the earlier patterns each line may represent either a single thread or a pair, but this is clearly indicated.

The bobbins and threads required are stated for each pattern. In most cases I have used Madeira Tanne 50 cotton, but the patterns can be enlarged to 120% if required, in which case they will require Madeira Tanne 30 cotton: Pattern 11 provides prickings in both sizes. In some cases alternative threads are given.

Bedfordshire lace and the Cluny connection

Bedfordshire lace evolved in the mid 19th Century in response to the advance of machine-made lace, the economic situation, and the fashion of the time. It retained elements of the East Midlands Point Ground lace, and incorporated Maltese and Honiton techniques. Major features were retained from the floral Point Ground lace, this having been the main competence of the designers. Its popularity was short-lived, however, because by 1865 lace machines were able to copy it. Although it continued to be made in Northamptonshire and Bedfordshire, it was a complex and time-consuming lace, and lace dealers would look elsewhere for patterns which would bring a quicker return.

An illustration of that search comes from the Northamptonshire village of Greens Norton where, at the turn of the century, a gentleman would travel to France each year in order to bring back new patterns for the local lace-makers.* These would probably have been Cluny patterns, which the workers would have found easier than fine floral Bedfordshire because of their simpler *geometric* designs and coarser threads.

Many simpler patterns now described as Bedfordshire are indistinguishable from Cluny patterns, but when a more intricate piece of floral Bedfordshire is attempted, the traditional Bedfordshire techniques that grew from Point Ground lace are required to achieve the best results. This applies to designs such as the Thomas Lester lace in the Cecil Higgins Art Gallery, Bedford, and to the work of other designers of the period which can be seen in the Luton and Northampton Museums. This mixture of patterns under a common name may be responsible for a certain confusion over the techniques actually used.

The basic difference of technique comes from the design. Cluny is a geometric lace with many crossings which are worked at a precise angle. Bedfordshire lace is a floral lace with the flow which comes from natural forms, and there is a boldness in the design which makes it stand out from its ground. Cluny lace is worked with a set number of threads, whereas Bedfordshire needs threads adding and removing to achieve the best effects. The three main techniques required are now described.

The trail The trail in Cluny lace normally has a constant number of threads, enabling it to be divided along parts of its central line by twisting the workers and/or passive pairs. When it does have a variable number of threads, that is a feature of the design and symmetry is maintained.**

In Bedfordshire lace, the trail is a vehicle to carry threads from one part of the pattern to another, so the number will vary though the eye perceives the trail to be the same width. The only difference between trails is that one may be a dominant design feature, and a narrower one joining it will be subsidiary (see Pl 11).

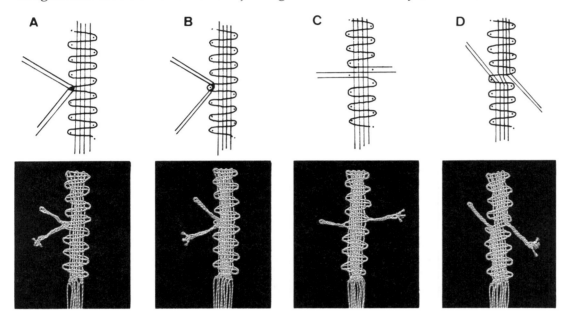

Plaits joining a trail or other part of the pattern In Cluny lace, where plaits join a trail and leave again immediately, the worker pair from the trail is exchanged for a pair from the plait, giving a tidy but flat effect (Fig A).

In Bedfordshire lace, the worker pair from the trail works through the plait pairs and back again after a pin is placed. The plait pairs briefly become part of the fabric of the trail, giving the effect of the ground continuing behind the trail (Fig B).

Plaits joining and leaving a trail When a plait joins a trail in Cluny lace, one pair can pass straight through it to leave directly at the other side, together with the worker pair. The second plait pair thus becomes the new worker pair (Fig C).

In Bedfordshire lace, it is unlikely that a plait would leave a trail directly opposite the join of another plait. A joining pair remains on the same side of the trail while a leaving pair leaves from its own side (Fig D).

* *Greens Norton, Rural Reflections*, Greens Norton [Northamptonshire] 50+ Club, no date.
** Paulis L & Rutgers M, *Technique & Design of Cluny Lace*, Ruth Bean, Bedford, 1984.

10

Using the book

Structure of the course

The intention of this book is to provide a thorough, step by step, grounding in the techniques of traditional Bedfordshire lace, including Bedfordshire Floral lace. By working systematically through the 20 graded lessons the lace-maker should acquire the skills to work traditional Bedfordshire lace independently.

Familiarity with the basics of bobbin lace-making is assumed, though a resumé of the stitches is provided in the next section.

The 20 lessons

Each lesson is constructed round a pattern and a piece (or pieces) of worked lace and combines new features with those learnt already. This allows the lace-maker to consolidate techniques and to practice new ones.

New techniques are listed at the beginning of each lesson and explained later in detail under the heading *Techniques*. They can be applied to any pattern. Working instructions then follow for the particular pattern. They include *Setting in and working the first head*, *Working the corner* (when applicable), and *Finishing*.

Working instructions for the earlier patterns are given in considerable detail, but this is gradually reduced until the lace-maker can work the last pattern with just a few tips.

Patterns are either copies of old prickings and drafts, or new designs with traditional features. The prickings chosen are quite small so that the lace-maker need not work a large piece of lace just to practise another technique.

Bobbins and threads

The number of bobbins required is given for the majority of patterns, though in a few of the more advanced ones this can only be approximate. By that stage the lace-maker will be able to decide whether to leave out pairs no longer required (by laying them to the back of the pillow) and add new ones for the next section, or to keep and re-use pairs already in the lace.

I have used cotton thread, Madeira Tanne 50 or 30, to work the lace. Samples were worked as indicated for each pattern. If the 50 thread seems too fine the pricking can be enlarged by 20% and the Tanne 30 used instead. Suggestions for alternative threads are also given.

Illustrations and lettering

Photos of the worked samples show the lace both actual size and enlarged $1\frac{1}{2}$ times. Finished pieces are displayed in colour at the centre of the book.

Each lesson has detailed diagrams illustrating the text, both for general techniques and for working the lace. The numbering of photographs and diagrams is related to each pattern, e.g. plates and figures for Pattern 9 are numbered Pl 9a, Fig 9a, etc.

In the diagrams each line represents one thread, unless otherwise stated. When there are too many pairs together to be shown clearly a line is used to represent a pair. These diagrams are marked (prs).

Numbers are used to show either how many pairs should be added at a pin-hole, or the order of working a section. Different subscript numbers added to the same pin-hole letter, e.g. T_1 & T_2 or F & F_1, indicate that the working of these pin-holes is connected in some way, as described in the text. T means 'temporary pin'.

The lettering has two functions. It shows the alphabetical order in which the pin-holes are to be worked and the correct position of the pillow for working a particular section. At a corner, for example, the letter is turned, and the pillow should also be turned, so that the lace-maker faces the letter straight on to work the pin-hole.

Whenever possible pin-holes related to a letter have been enlarged to show they are linked.

Prickings

Prickings are shown actual size at the end. In round patterns the starting point is suggested by an arrow. All medallions, including the oval in Pattern 13, are started at the top and worked down.

Additional prickings are provided for any lace shown in the colour centre spread which is not included in the lessons: threads used to make them are given in the caption.

Equipment and basic techniques

Materials

The pillow Use a round, slightly domed pillow, 18 to 20 in (50 cm) in diameter, made of straw or polystyrene, covered in strong, dark blue or green lint-free material. You also need a cover cloth of the same material, approx. 20 in (50 cm) square, to be secured across the pricking, just below the area being worked, to enable the bobbins to move smoothly from side to side. Make sure the square has a selvage, and pin it at the top to prevent excessive wear on the threads (see Diag). A second cloth is needed to cover the work when not in use and keep it free from dust.

The pricking You will need glazed card, a cork board and a pin-vice containing a No 9 needle.

Photocopy or trace the required pattern. Cut the card a little larger than the pattern, allowing about ¼ in (6 mm) all the way round. Lay it on the board and place the pattern on top; a piece of plastic coated carbon paper may be placed between the two to help with the marking out. Pin down firmly at the corners onto the board with drawing pins. Prick through each dot, holding the pin-vice *upright*. The needle may be lubricated with beeswax if necessary.

If you have used a carbon layer draw over all the design markings with a sharp pencil before removing from the board. Remove from the board and re-mark the design-lines on the glazed card with a fine black marking pen.

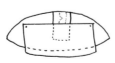
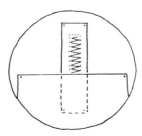

Bobbins Bobbins for Bedfordshire lace may be made of bone, wood or plastic. They must have a spangle, a ring of beads, to provide the right tension and prevent the bobbins rolling over the work. Bobbins are wound in pairs.

Follow Figs *a*, *b* & *c*. Holding a bobbin in the left hand, wind the thread onto the neck as shown until it is firm, then continue by twisting the bobbin and drawing the thread straight from the reel. Wind the thread only up to the collar of the bobbin. Secure the thread by a hitch round the head of the bobbin: fold the thread back on itself as shown in Figs *a* & *b*, and wind it 3 times round the head as shown in Figs *b* & *c*. Pull the loop firmly to lock it in position. Now draw a length of thread and wind its end onto the second bobbin in the same way, joining them together and leaving a few inches of thread between them.

To release the thread turn the bobbin towards the left.

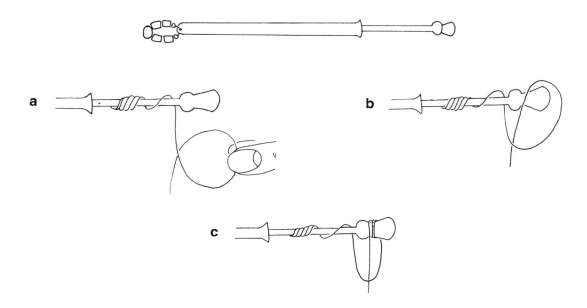

Thread Traditionally Bedfordshire lace was made with linen thread which gave it its characteristic crispness. The linen threads available today can still be used for the coarser patterns. For the finer patterns cotton must be used, since fine linen threads are not generally available.

Cotton threads are available with varying degrees of twisting, from the highly twisted to the softer ones. Working plaits and tallies puts strain on the thread. A softly twisted thread makes good plaits and tallies but lacks the strength required for a strong fabric. A highly twisted thread on the other hand, though strong, is not pliable enough to make good plaits and tallies. A cotton thread with a medium twist is recommended, and alternative threads are suggested.

Silk threads, which combine both flexibility and strength, are also available. They offer in addition a range of magnificent colours, as can be seen on the cover and the centre plate. As Maltese, one of the 'forebears' of Bedfordshire lace, was frequently made in silk, there is good reason to encourage its use. Moreover, had there been suitable coloured threads in the 19th Century, lace-makers would certainly have used them too. Working our lace in colour, as well as in white, enlivens and enhances this traditional craft and we should encourage it.

Pins Medium to fine strong pins are required for Bedfordshire lace. When placing pins make those on the sides slope outwards and backwards, and those in the middle slope backwards, all at the same angle.

Leave in the pins at the beginning of the work and at the edges for as long as possible; those in the middle of the pattern may be brought forward from the back and used for new work, always leaving about 2 in (5 cm) pinned securely.

The stitches

Bedfordshire lace is worked *with the right side up* and is made with two stitches: *cloth stitch* and *half-stitch*. Variations are created by putting twists between the stitches. All stitches are worked with two pairs of bobbins (4 threads). Two movements are used to create the stitches, a *cross* and a *twist*.

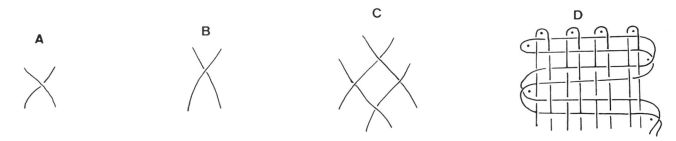

Cross Diag A A cross is made by passing the left-hand thread over the right-hand thread. In Bedfordshire lace the cross is only used as part of the cloth stitch and the half-stitch, unlike the twist which has other functions as well.

Twist Diag B A twist is made by passing the right-hand thread of a pair over the left-hand thread. Twists are used:

a. to make the cloth stitch and the half-stitch; b. to hold threads apart; c. to fill spaces where two separate threads would be untidy; d. to keep the lace fabric firm; e. for decoration.

The number of twists on a pair is marked on the diagrams by short cross lines (see Pattern markings).

Cloth stitch Diags C & D Cross centre left thread over centre right; twist both pairs once; cross centre left thread over centre right. This completes a cloth stitch.

Diagram *D* shows cloth stitches worked in rows. One pair works a cloth stitch with each pair hanging down in a row and is called the *worker pair*. The hanging threads are called the *passives*.

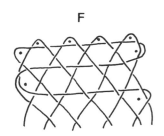

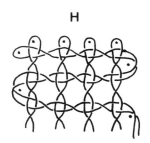

At the end of each row the worker pair is twisted and a pin is placed in the pin-hole; it is then worked back making the same movements. Rows of cloth stitch are normally worked at 90° to the right-hand edge of the lace, the footside.

14

Half-stitch Diags *E* & *F*   Cross the centre left thread over the centre right; twist both pairs. Diagram *F* shows the half-stitch worked in rows. Only one thread works across all the hanging or passive threads, which must be left crossed as shown.

Cloth stitch and twist (Whole stitch) Diags *G* & *H*   Follow the movements for cloth stitch, then twist both pairs once. Diagram *H* shows cloth stitch and twist worked in rows. The footside is sometimes worked in this stitch.

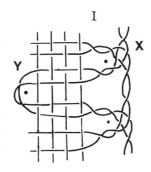

The Footside Diag *I*   The footside is an important feature in Bedfordshire lace and is a straight edge on the right-hand side of the pattern. It usually has 2 or 3 pairs of passives but can contain more pairs if the pattern requires it.

At the outer edge pin-hole, *x*, the worker pair changes places with the edge pair, as follows.

Work up to, but not including the edge pair. Twist the workers twice and place the pin under them. Work a cloth stitch with the edge pair and twist both pairs twice pulling the stitch up closely to the pin. The second pair from the edge becomes the new worker pair.

The number of twists on the outer edge pair will vary according to the vertical space to be filled.

At the inner edge pin-hole, *y*, when no pairs are taken in or left out, the workers are twisted 2 to 4 times and held in position by the pin. This is called a *winkie pin*. The thinner the thread, the more twists are needed to fill the space and hold the passive pairs firmly together.

The footside can also be worked in cloth stitch and twist (Diag *H*), but not when pairs need to be carried in it to another part of the pattern.

Pattern markings

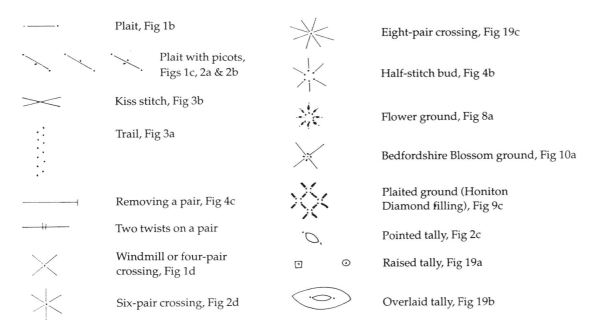

Plait, Fig 1b	Eight-pair crossing, Fig 19c
Plait with picots, Figs 1c, 2a & 2b	Half-stitch bud, Fig 4b
Kiss stitch, Fig 3b	Flower ground, Fig 8a
Trail, Fig 3a	Bedfordshire Blossom ground, Fig 10a
Removing a pair, Fig 4c	Plaited ground (Honiton Diamond filling), Fig 9c
Two twists on a pair	Pointed tally, Fig 2c
Windmill or four-pair crossing, Fig 1d	Raised tally, Fig 19a
Six-pair crossing, Fig 2d	Overlaid tally, Fig 19b

Where to start

The starting points for the patterns in this book are indicated by an arrow where it is not already clear.

If you later tackle a new pricking for a border, however, it is better to think first where you want to *finish* rather than where you should start. You need a firm edge to attach the ends, and a staggered line will distract the eye from a join more readily than a straight one.

It is difficult to camouflage a join in the ground unless you are an expert needlewoman, so pick a position with the smallest amount of ground. When working a square edging a good place is just before or after a corner, since the eye tends to look at the corner or further down the side.

Reading list

Buck, A, *Thomas Lester, his Lace and the East Midlands Industry 1820-1905*, Bedford, 1981.
Channer, C.C., and Buck, A, *In the cause of English Lace*, Bedford, 1991.
Cole, A. S, *Report on Northampton, Bucks and Beds Lace-making*, 1892.
Freeman, C, *Pillow Lace in the East Midlands*, Luton, 1958.
Wright, T, *The Romance of the Lace Pillow, Olney*, 1919; 2nd edition 1924: reprint Bedford, 1982.
Underwood, B, *Traditional Bedfordshire Lace*, Bedford 1988.

Pattern 1
Border with ninepin edge

The ninepin edge is a traditional design commonly found on the headside of Bedfordshire patterns. It is usually learnt as a first step in Bedfordshire lace techniques.

Introducing Three ways of hanging pairs to begin work, the plait, the left-hand picot, the windmill crossing, using a pin-hole twice, moving or 'lifting' the lace back on the pricking (setting up), finishing a border.

Materials 8 pairs of bobbins: Madeira Tanne 30

Techniques

Hanging pairs on fixed pins and on temporary pins to begin work, Fig 1a The following are the common methods of hanging in pairs to set in a piece of lace.

a. As a general rule, at marked pin-holes, 2 pairs are hung, *straddled* (Fig 1a,i). Twist them once and enclose the pin with a cloth stitch. Each pair will then work in a different direction.

b. Another method for fixed pins is to lay two pairs from the back to the front of the pillow (Fig 1a,ii), to one side of a pin-hole. The two threads hanging towards the lace-maker are treated as a

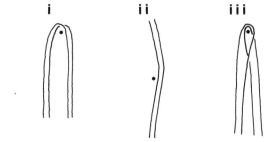

Fig 1a *Three methods of hanging in pairs*

Methods i-ii are used mainly to hang in pairs on fixed pins: method iii to hang pairs on temporary pins, used mainly to set in trails.

i Two pairs hung *straddled* on a pin.
ii Pairs are hung *from the back to the front of the pillow*. To incorporate the pairs into the lace, follow instructions for pin-hole B in Fig 1g.
iii Two pairs hung *side by side* on a temporary pin.

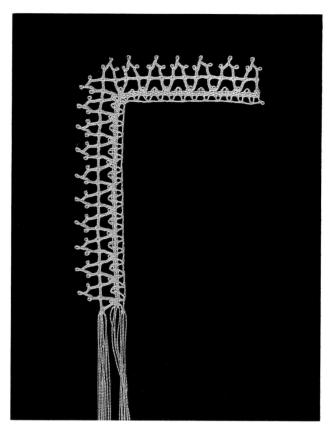

Pl 1

pair of passives. Work through this pair with the worker pair (see below, pin-hole B, Fig 1g); place the pin and work through it again. This will anchor the pairs round the pin. Bring together the four threads of the pairs and work a plait, as shown.

c. On temporary pins a varying number of pairs can be hung, normally *side by side*. After the pairs have been worked through for several rows, remove the temporary pin and ease the pairs down into position: they will lie side by side as passives.

The plait, Fig 1b A plait or leg is a short bar, used as a component of the decorative ninepin edge, or of the ground, and for joining different parts of the design. It is made with 2 pairs working a continuous half-stitch between two pin-holes.

After every 2 or 3 stitches, gently pull each thread separately to tighten the plait and make it lie flat. Continue until the space between the pin-holes is filled, with the pin-hole towards which you are working still visible.

17

Fig 1b
The plait

Made in a continuous line of half-stitch. Pull each threads gently after a few stitches to tighten and make it lie flat.

The left-hand picot, Fig 1c Plaits are often decorated with small loops or picots, which can be on the left, right or both sides of the plait. Their position is marked by a pin-hole. In this pattern they are on the left.

Work the plait until it is almost level with the pin-hole. Twist the left-hand pair 3 times. From the outside, insert a pin under the left thread of the pair (1c,i); twist it forward and outward to the left (1c,ii) and place it in the pin-hole (1c,iii). Do not tighten the thread.

Bring the second thread of the pair to the left and loop it clockwise round the back of the pin (1c,iv); tighten both threads together and twist them twice (1c,v).

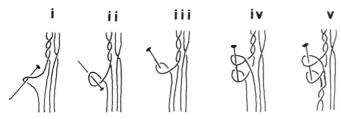

i	ii	iii	iv	v

Fig 1c   *Left-hand picot*

i   Insert a pin under the left-hand thread.
ii Twist the pin forward and outward to the left.
iii Place the pin.
iv Loop the second thread clockwise round the back of the pin.
v   Tighten both threads together, twist twice.

The windmill or 4-pair crossing, Fig 1d A crossing is a point of anchorage where four or more pairs are worked through each other in order to hold a section of the lace together. In this pattern pairs from two plaits cross each other. Each pair is used as one thread and worked in cloth stitch with a pin placed at its centre.

Cross centre-left pair *a* over centre-right pair *b*. Twist both pairs once; place the pin. Cross centre-left pair *c* over centre-right pair *d*.

Moving or 'lifting' the lace back on the pricking (setting up) When you get to the end of the pricking you may have to lift the lace and re-pin it at the beginning to obtain the desired length.

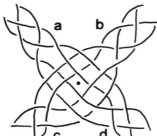

Fig 1d
Windmill crossing

Work a cloth stitch using each pair as a thread. Place a support pin in the centre.

Wrap and pin the cover cloth firmly round the bobbins so that they remain secure. Holding the bundle of bobbins very carefully in one hand, take out the pins from the lace with the other. Lift the work off the pillow and position the last 2 or 3 heads of the lace over the corresponding pin-holes at the beginning of the pricking. Carefully re-pin the heads into the matching pin-holes. Repeat if necessary.

Working the lace

Photocopy the pattern and prick it onto glazed card. Draw the lines marking the positions of the plaits. Pin the card firmly onto the pillow. Cover the bottom half of the pricking with a cloth. Make sure the selvage is at the top so that the bobbins can move freely from side to side without wearing the threads.

Setting in and working the first head, Figs 1a & 1e-1h Start at the footside. Hang 2 pairs of bobbins, *straddled*, over the pin at *A*: these will be the edge pairs. Hang 2 pairs, *side by side*, over a temporary pin T_1 between *A* & *B*: these will be the footside passive pairs. Hang 2 pairs, *from the back to the front of the pillow*, to the right of *B*: these pairs will work the ninepin.

Twist the right-hand pair at *A* once and work a cloth stitch with the two pairs. Twist the outer pair 3 times and the inner pair twice. The inner pair will be the worker pair. With the worker pair, work to the left in cloth stitch, through the 3 pairs: 2 passives and 1 laying on the right of pin-hole *B*. Twist the workers once, place pin *B*.

Work to the right in cloth stitch, through the 3 pairs; twist twice, place edge pin *C*. Work a cloth stitch with the workers and the outer pair, twist the outer pair 3 times and the inner pair (now the new worker pair) twice. Work in cloth stitch to the left, through two pairs, twist the worker pair 3 times, place pin *D*. Continue in cloth stitch to the next edge pin *E*.

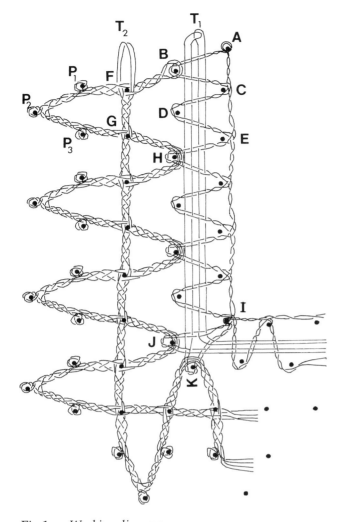

Fig 1e   *Working diagram*

Remove the temporary pin T_1 and gently pull down the threads for the footside passives.

Return to pin *B* (Fig 1g) and the two pairs hung from back to front, which were already worked through twice by the worker pair from *A*. Bring the threads from the back of the pillow forward to those lying at the front, twist both pairs once, and work a plait to pin-hole *F* (Figs 1e & 1g).

Hang 2 more pairs, straddled, on a temporary pin T_2, above pin *F* (Fig 1h). With these pairs and the plait pairs from *B* work a windmill crossing at *F*. Remove temporary pin T_2 and with these new pairs make a plait to *G* and leave to one side.

Return to the windmill crossing at *F* and make a plait to the first picot pin-hole P_1. Make a left-hand picot (follow Fig 1c). Continue making plaits and picots to pin-holes P_2, P_3 & *G*, pulling the plait together very tightly after each picot. At *G* work a windmill crossing with the plait pairs

from *F*. Continue by making a plait to *H* where it will join the footside (Fig 1e) as follows.

With the footside worker from *E* work to the left in cloth stitch, through the two passive pairs, and through the plait pairs from *G*. Twist the worker twice and place pin *H*. This completes one ninepin. Work back to the right, through the plait pairs and the passives, leaving out the two plait pairs at *H* to start the next ninepin.

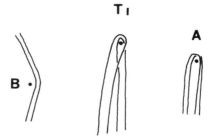

Fig 1f   *Setting in*

Pin-hole *A*: Hang two pairs, straddled. Pin-hole *B*: Hang two pairs from the back to the front of the pillow to the right of *B* to work a plait to the left. Temporary pin T_1: Hang two pairs, side by side, for the trail passives.

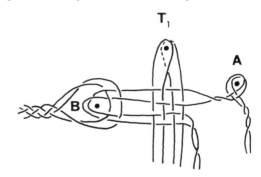

Fig 1g   *Setting in the footside*

Working pin-holes *A*, *B* and T_1.

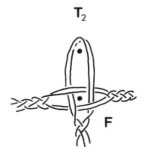

Fig 1h   *Setting in the headside*

Hang 2 pairs on a temporary pin and work a windmill crossing at pin-hole *F*.

19

Taking or joining pairs into another part of a pattern, and letting them leave immediately to the same side, is a feature of traditional Bedfordshire lace (see Pattern 3, Fig 3a). Continue working in this way up to pin-hole *I*, remembering that the last one or two inches of worked lace must always be secured with pins to maintain the shape and tension.

Working the corner, Fig 1e Work the lace until you have completed pin-holes *I* & *J* and the two ninepin heads at the corner. Turn the pillow as necessary so that you always work down towards you.

Pl 1a   *Enlarged section of Pl 1*

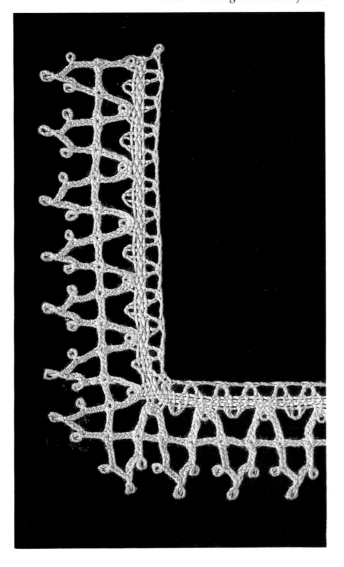

Use the footside worker that has completed pin-hole *J* to work back through the first of the footside passives and become a passive pair for the next footside. The pair just worked through will be the worker pair for the next footside. Place pin *K*. Work across two pairs of passives. Twist the worker pair twice; untwist the outer pair. Remove the pin from pin-hole *I* and re-pin into the same pin-hole, *under* the worker pair. Work a cloth stitch with the worker pair and the outer pair, twist the outer pair 3 times and the inner pair (the worker pair) twice. The technique of using a pin-hole twice makes a neater corner.

Finishing, Fig 1i The beginning and the end of the lace will be joined by a series of sewings. First, pin the beginning of the work back onto the pillow against the ending, so that the last pin-holes worked match and meet those of the first. Each pair of bobbins at the end of the work must correspond to a loop at the beginning. The two parts will be joined by a *sewing* as shown in the diagram. Using a very fine crochet hook make a loop with one thread of a pair through the matching loop at the beginning of the lace. Insert the second thread of the pair through the loop so formed. Repeat with each pair of threads. Knot each pair separately and either oversew the ends or thread them back neatly into the work.

Fig 1i   *A sewing*

Stitch for joining the beginning and end of a border.

Pattern 2

Insertion and border with pointed tallies

The pattern has been adapted from an old scrap of lace. It has been chosen for this lesson because its main feature, the pointed tally, is an important part of Bedfordshire lace. Two patterns are given: one, like the old piece, is an insertion; the other has been made into an edging with a corner.

With a little practice, making tallies becomes very satisfying, though you mustn't expect perfection at the first attempt!

Introducing Right-hand & double picots, the pointed tally, the six-pair crossing, adding pairs by a 'false picot' and removing pairs at a corner (Pattern 2b).

Materials Insertion, 8 pairs of bobbins; border, 10 pairs: Madeira Tanne 30.

Techniques

Right-hand & double picots, Figs 2a & 2b Work the plait until almost up to the picot pin-hole. Twist the right-hand pair 3 times. Follow Fig 2a.

From the outside, insert a pin under the right-hand thread, twist it forward, then outward to the right (Fig 2a,i-iii). Place the pin without tightening the thread. Bring the left-hand thread first to the right and then round the back of the pin, anti-clockwise, tightening the two threads together. Twist them twice (Fig 2a,iv&v).

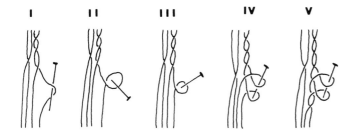

Fig 2a *Right-hand picot*

i   Insert a pin under the right-hand thread.
ii Twist the pin forward and outward to the right.
iii Place the pin.

iv Loop the second thread anti-clockwise round the back of the pin.
v Tighten both threads together, twist twice.

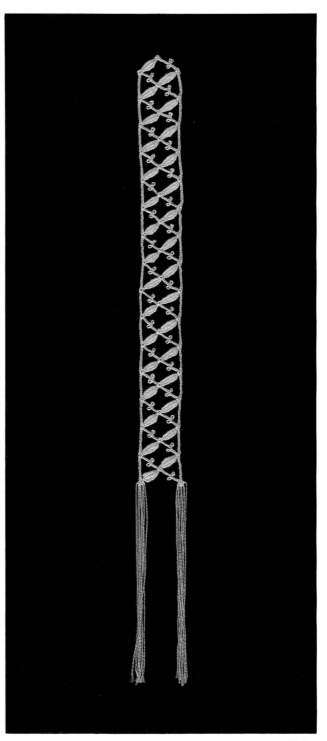

Pl 2

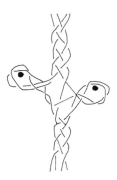

Fig 2b   *Plait with double picot*

First work the picot further up the pricking, then a half-stitch with the two pairs before making the second picot.

Double picots are shown on the pricking by pin-holes on either side of a (solid) plait line. First work the one with the pin-hole higher on the pricking, like the left-hand one in Fig 2b, and make a half stitch between it and the second picot.

Fig 2c   *Pointed or leaf-shaped tally*

The pointed tally, Fig 2c Tallies, also called 'leaves', 'plaits' or 'lead-works', are small solid blocks of weaving, common in Bedfordshire patterns. They can be leaf-shaped (pointed), square or rectangular and form different parts of the design. The most common tally is the leaf-shaped or pointed tally shown in this pattern.

These tallies are worked between two pin-holes, with two pairs hanging from a pin. One of the four threads is woven over and under the other three.

Follow Fig 2c. Enclose the pin with a cloth stitch and take the second thread from the right as the single worker thread.

Hold the three passive threads well apart and weave the worker thread under and over them, from side to side, as shown. *Do not let go of the worker until the tally is finished*, and keep the passives well apart until you are half-way down the

tally. Gradually bring the passives closer together, all the while weaving over and under. The shape is formed by tensioning the worker. Make the tally long enough to reach the next pin-hole, or a fraction further. Place the pin between the pairs and gently pull the three passive threads. This will tighten the tally to fit the space; finish with a cloth stitch.

Don't worry if at first you make what might look like holly leaves; you just need a bit of practice!

The six-pair crossing, Fig 2d   As with the wind-mill crossing, each pair is counted as one thread. Work as follows.

Pair 2 over 3; pair 4 over 5; pair 4 over 3; pair 2 over 3; pair 4 over 5; pair 2 over 1; pair 6 over 5; pair 2 over 3; pair 4 over 5; place the pin; pair 4 over 3; pair 2 over 3; pair 4 over 5.

Follow the diagram and the list of moves. Get someone to read it out to you as you work. At the end, pull all threads very firmly before continuing.

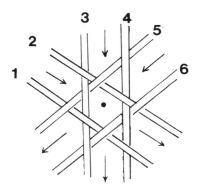

Fig 2d   *Six-pair crossing*

Pattern 2a

The insertion

Working the lace

Setting in and working the first head, Figs 2e-g
Prepare the pricking as directed for Pattern 1. Wind 8 pairs of bobbins.

Place 2 temporary pins above pin-hole *A* and hang 2 pairs, straddled, on each. Work a windmill crossing at *A* (Fig 2e). Remove the temporary pins and ease the threads down into place.

With the two right-hand pairs work a plait to the picot pin-holes (Fig 2f). Work a double picot, first the right-hand one (it is higher on the pricking), then a half-stitch and the left-hand picot. Continue working the plait to *B*. With the two left-hand pairs at *A*, work a tally to *C*.

Place temporary pins above *B* and *C*. Hang 2 pairs, straddled, on each. With the new pairs and those already in the lace, work a windmill crossing at both *B* and *C*. Remove the temporary pins and ease the threads down into place.

With the two pairs that worked the plait from *A* to *B*, make the outer right-hand plait to *D*. With the two pairs that made the tally from *A* to *C* work the outer left-hand plait to *E*. With the new pairs at *B* make a tally to *F*, and with the new pairs at *C* make a plait with double picots, to *F*. Work a windmill crossing at *F* and continue in this way down the pricking.

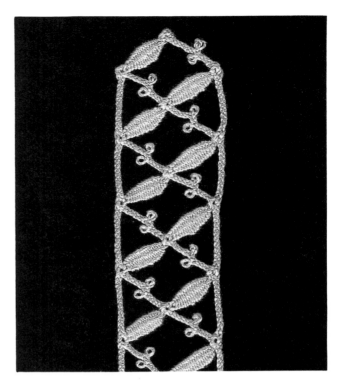

Pl 2a   *Enlarged section of Pl 2*

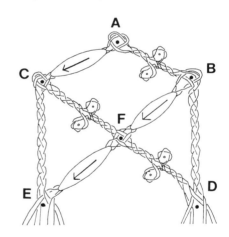

Fig 2g   *Working diagram for insertion*

Finishing   The insertion can be finished either on a point, to match the beginning, or on a straight line across the lace, as shown in Pl 2a.

Finishing on a point   Work the windmill crossing at the centre, knot together the outer plait pairs and each two adjacent pairs. Allow thread for a tassel as shown on the cover bookmark.

Finishing across the lace   Work to the outer pin-holes as at *D* and *E* (Fig 2g), knotting the pairs on either side as shown in the Plate. Cut the threads as desired.

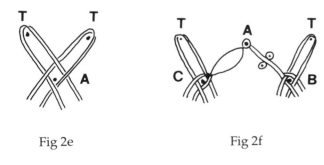

Fig 2e   Fig 2f

Fig 2e   Setting in pin A

Hang pairs for pin *A* using temporary pins and work a windmill crossing.

Fig 2f   Setting in pins B & C using temporary pins and windmill crossings

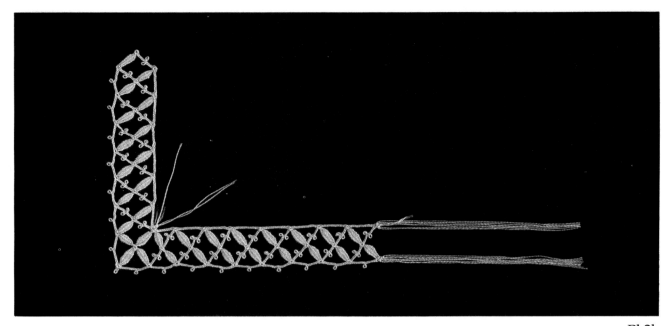

Pattern 2b

Border with pointed tallies

The pattern provides an exercise in working a simple corner by adding 2 pairs. The pairs are added at the outer edge and the technique is sometimes known as a *false picot*.

The exercise also shows that a picot, added to the edge of an insertion, can turn the edge into a headside.

Working the lace

Setting in, Fig 2h   Set in and work the pattern in the same way as the insertion, except that between C and E you must work a left-hand picot to create the headside.

Work down to the corner line G-J in the order indicated by the arrows.

Note that the plait from the headside to pinhole I has changed into a tally. Turn the pillow.

Working the corner, Figs 2h & 2i   Two extra pairs are needed to work the corner line, from G to J. Hang these 2 pairs, straddled, on a pin at G and twist 4 times. Work a cloth stitch and twist each pair twice. This is sometimes called a *false picot*.

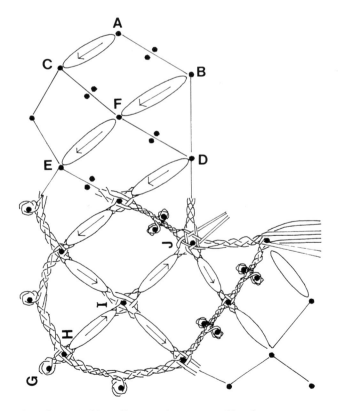

Fig 2h   *Working diagram for corner of border*

24

With the new pairs and those from the edge plait work a windmill crossing at *H* (Fig 2i).

Continue with the new pairs and, following the arrows on Fig 2h, work a tally to *I*, then a windmill crossing at *I* and a tally to pin-hole *J*

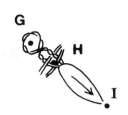

Fig 2i   *Setting in the corner line at G*

Two pairs added at pin G using a 'false picot' will work the corner line and be removed at the inner corner.

At pin-hole *J* work a six-pair crossing (Fig 2d). Remove the pairs you added at *G* by laying them to the back of the pillow. Before cutting off the bobbins leave enough thread so they can be knotted together and sewn into the lace with a needle, or later sewn into the fabric during mounting.

Setting up   Follow instructions in Pattern 1 for lifting the lace and re-pinning it to the head of the pricking.

Finishing   To finish the lace, follow instructions in Pattern 1.

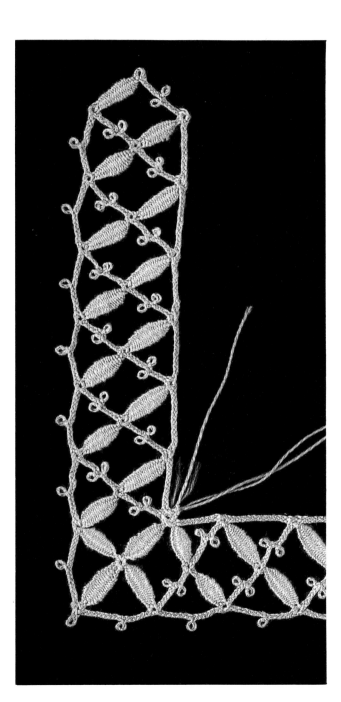

Pl 2c   *Enlarged section of Pl 2b*

Two extra pairs were added at the outer corner by a 'false picot' and removed at the inner corner.

25

Pattern 3

Circular border with parallel trails

This pattern lets you practice the techniques learned so far and try some new ones as well, in particular joining together separate parts of a pattern.

Note the double bar to the ninepin edge, which makes it firmer, and easier to launder. The footside has only one pair of passives and is worked with a cloth stitch and twist.

Introducing Working a circular border, the double-bar ninepin edge, the main and secondary trails, the winkie pin, joining pairs to a trail, the kiss stitch and its use in joining the trail to the footside.

Materials 18 pairs of bobbins: Madeira Tanne 30, or Linen 90 or 100.

Techniques

Working a circular border The general rule that cloth stitch areas must always be worked at 90° to the footside cannot be followed strictly here as this is a circular pattern. However, the general direction of the work must be downwards, towards the lace-maker. The pillow must be turned regularly to maintain the correct angle and keep

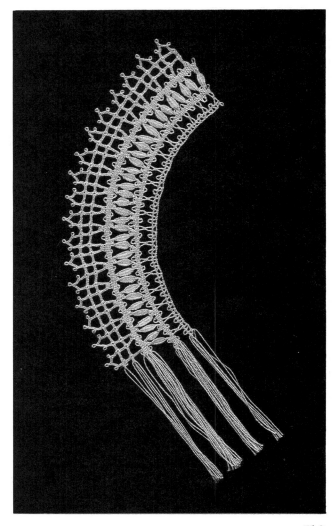

Pl 3

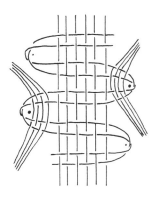

Fig 3a *Taking plait pairs into a trail*

The pairs leave immediately on the same side.

the passive pairs as near parallel to the footside edge as possible. To keep your bearings imagine that the centre of the circle is an extension of the footside, and use the radius line as a guide for the working rows. It is also helpful to place the cover cloth on this line, and move it frequently.

The trail, Fig 3a Most Bedfordshire patterns have at least a main trail, which is worked in cloth stitch, and often a secondary trail. A trail is like a footside without the edge pair.

The number of passive pairs throughout a trail can vary but the eye will not notice this unless there are so many they produce a seersucker effect, or so few that the design is lost.

Work in cloth stitch from side to side, across the passive pairs. At the edge pin-holes work 'winkie pins'.

26

The winkie pin, Fig 3a This is the loop formed by twisting the worker pair round the edge pin. The twisting will hold the cloth stitch firmly together and give the trail its characteristic edge loops or *winkie pins*. Winkie pins are also worked on the inner edge of footside trails and in other areas of cloth-work, such as leaves and flowers.

Twist the worker pair twice (or more if required by the pattern), place the edge pin and continue to the next pin-hole.

Joining (plait) pairs to a trail, Fig 3a With the worker pair work in cloth stitch through the joining pairs (mostly two), twist 2-3 times, place the pin, work through them again and continue the trail. The pairs just worked through can either become part of the trail or be left out again immediately on the same side, as shown.

The kiss stitch, Fig 3b This is a joining stitch that connects two parts of a pattern by exchanging the worker pairs.

Twist each worker pair 3 times, work a cloth stitch and twist the pairs 3 more times. The worker pairs will have changed sides. The pinholes are only position markers, or used as props.

Fig 3b *Kiss stitch*

Worker pairs from adjacent parts of the pattern change places and form a join.

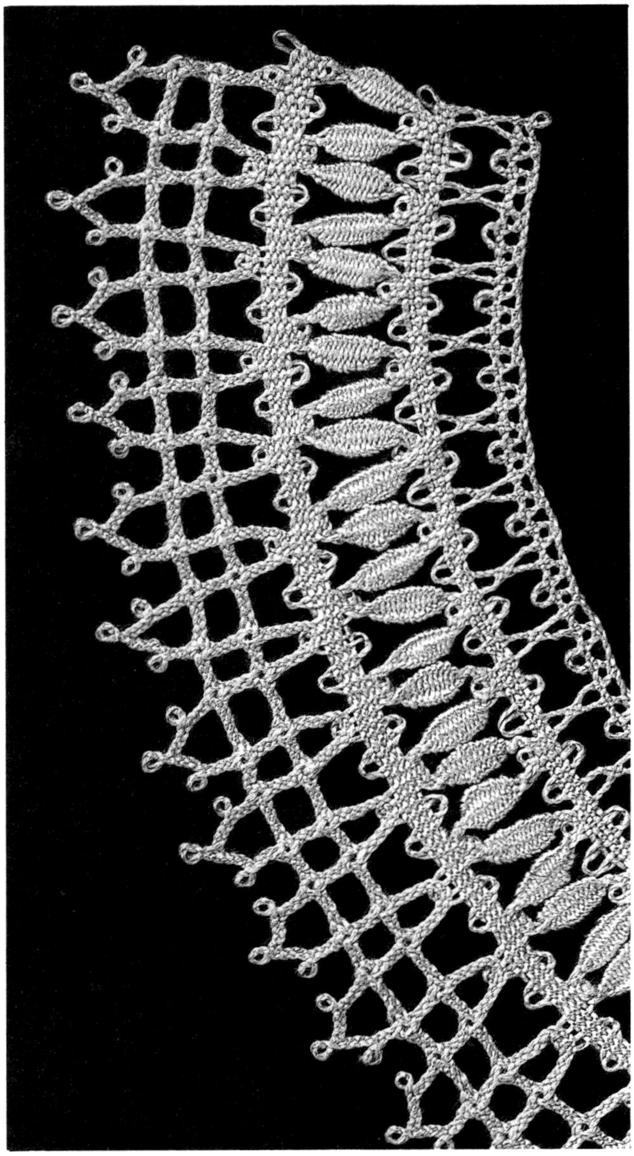

Pl 3a *Enlarged first section of Pl 3*

Working the lace

Setting in and working the first head, Fig 3c Prepare the pricking as directed for Pattern 1 and place the five temporary pins as shown.

Start with the main trail. Hang 3 pairs, side by side, on a temporary pin above pin-hole A: these are the passive pairs for the main trail. Hang 1 pair on a pin at A, to be the trail worker pair. With this pair work in cloth stitch to pin-hole B.

Before placing pin B, hang 2 pairs, from back to front of the pillow, to the left of pin-hole B (for the tally to I) and work a cloth stitch through the two threads, twist the workers once, place pin B. Work back in a cloth stitch through the threads at B again and the 3 passives, towards pin-hole C.

Before placing pin C, hang 2 pairs, from back to front of the pillow, to the right of pin-hole C. Work in cloth stitch through the two threads, twist once. Place pin C. Work back through the threads at C, the trail passives, but not through the pairs added at B; they are being left out to work the tally to I.

Leave the trail worker pair to one side, supported over a pin.

Return to the ninepin edge. Bring together the threads of the two pairs added at C, twist them once and make a plait to D, then work a windmill crossing with the pairs hanging, straddled, from the temporary pin above D. Remember to remove the temporary pin and ease down the threads. Work a plait to G and a plait from D to E.

Now work a windmill crossing, with the two pairs hanging, straddled, from a temporary pin above E. Place pin E and plait to pin-hole F.

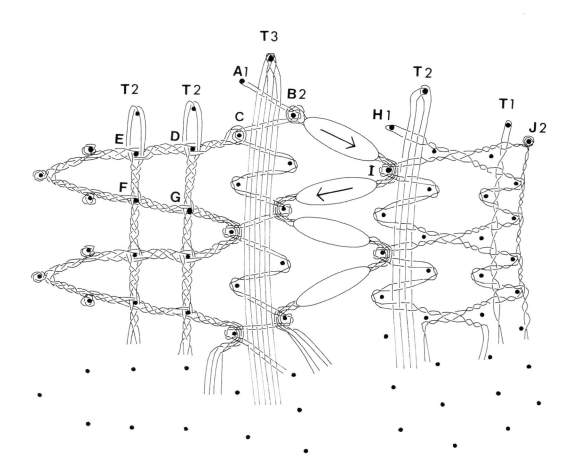

Fig 3c   *Working diagram*

Work the outer ninepin edge with its picots. Work a windmill at *F*, make a plait and windmill crossing at *G*. Continue the plait so that it reaches the main trail and leave aside.

Begin the secondary trail. Return to pin *B*. Bring together the threads of the two pairs added there and work a tally to reach the secondary trail at *I*. Hang one pair at *H* and work in cloth stitch through the two passive pairs hanging, side by side from a temporary pin above it. Twist 3 times (for the first half of the kiss stitch) and leave to one side, supported by a pin.

Begin the footside. With the two pairs, hung on pin *J*, work a cloth stitch and twist twice. With the left-hand pair and the passive pair, hanging from a temporary pin above *J*, work a cloth stitch. Twist the passive pair once. Twist the worker pair 3 times, place the second support pin and work a cloth stitch with the worker pair from the secondary trail waiting on a pin. Twist each pair 3 times. This completes the kiss stitch and the workers have changed places.

The left-hand worker pair now continues the secondary trail. Work in cloth stitch through the two passive pairs of the trail and the two pairs which have completed the tally. Twist the worker pair twice and place pin *I*. Work in cloth stitch through the tally pairs again and the passive pairs but leave the tally pairs out immediately on the same side to work the next tally. Continue in cloth stitch down the trail to the next kiss stitch.

Return to the footside. Use the right-hand worker pair from the first kiss stitch and the passive pair and work a cloth stitch. Twist the worker twice and the passive pair once. Place the edge pin. Work a cloth stitch with the edge pair; twist both pairs twice.

Continue in this way across and down the pattern until 2 to 3 in have been worked. Now push the first few pins worked well down into the pillow, also those at the inner and outer edge of the footside and at the outer edge of the ninepin head. The pins from the centre of the work may be taken out from the back and used for new work. It is only on curved edges that pins are pushed down into the pillow, because standing pins would get in the way.

Continue until all the pin-holes have been worked.

Finishing To finish the border follow instructions in Pattern 1.

Pattern 4

Bookmark with Bedfordshire bud and rounded ends

This pricking is adapted from an old pattern for a traditional Bedfordshire insertion. It provides an exercise in working a footside on either edge, with a simple trail for the top and bottom rounded edges. The tallies and plaits you have learned already are now combined with a new feature, the Bedfordshire bud.

Introducing Setting in on a curved edge to work in both directions, the Bedfordshire half-stitch bud, removing pairs by. laying them to the back of the pillow, finishing on a curve, finishing on a point.

Materials 16 pairs of bobbins: Madeira Tanne 30, or Retors d'Alsace 30, or Linen 80 or 90, or Gutterman silk, or Mulberry silk fine.

Techniques

***Setting in on a curved edge to work in both directions**, Figs 4a & 4e* Hang 6 pairs from side to side across the pillow to provide 3 passive pairs for each side. At *a* hang 2 more pairs on a pin and twist twice; these will be the worker pairs for either side. With one pair work in cloth stitch through the passive pairs to *b*, and with the other to *c*.

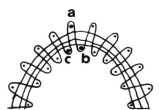

Fig 4a *Setting in on a curved edge*

The letters show the order of setting in the edge trail. (prs)

***The Bedfordshire half-stitch bud**, Fig 4b* The bud is worked entirely in half-stitch with plait pairs coming in for the upper half and being left out from the lower half.
  Place the pin at *a*, between the two pairs of the plait, and work a half-stitch. Continue in half-

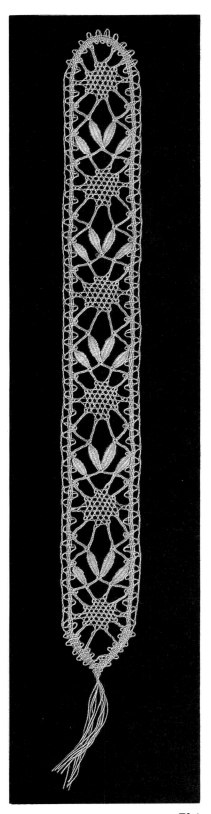

PI 4

30

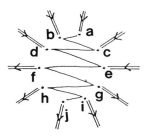

Fig 4b   *Bedfordshire half-stitch bud* (prs)

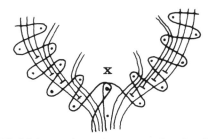

Fig 4d   *Finishing an insertion on a point.* (prs)

stitch to either side up to the next highest pin-hole, in this case to *b*. Work in half-stitch across the waiting plait pairs, add an extra twist on the workers, and place pin *b*.

Work in half-stitch from pin-hole to pin-hole, putting an extra twist on the workers before placing the pin. Take in waiting pairs from the plaits up to half-way through the bud, and leave out 2 pairs at each pin-hole in the second half.

***Removing pairs by laying them to the back of the pillow**, Fig 4c* Where the diagram shows a blocked-off line it means that a pair is no longer needed and is to be laid to the back of the pillow and cut off later. Although the lines represent pairs, a better result is obtained by removing *alternate threads*, which will avoid holes forming in the lace. Leave 2 to 3 in of thread and cut off the bobbins. When *all pins* have been removed cut off these threads, one by one, close to the lace.

***Finishing on a curve**, Fig 4c* Tie together firmly the threads remaining at the end and weave them back into the lace with a needle, or sew them through the backing fabric if the piece is being mounted.

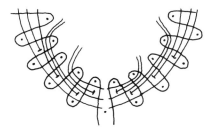

Fig 4c   *Finishing an insertion on a curve*

Pairs are removed from the trail by laying to the back of the pillow. Remaining pairs are knotted together. (prs)

***Finishing on a point**, Fig 4d* Bring the workers from either side to pin-hole *x*. Twist both once, work a cloth stitch, twist, place the pin, and work another cloth stitch. Leave one pair as a passive: with the other pair work in cloth stitch to the side from which they came, and then backward and forward through the rest of the passives, to any remaining pin-holes. Having done this, plait the remaining threads to the desired length or tie a thread round them to form a tassel.

Working the lace

***Setting in and working the edges**, Figs 4e-4h* Lay 6 pairs across the top of the pillow and anchor them to one side with a pin A_1. They will be the passive pairs: 3 pairs for the left-hand side and 3 for the right. Anchor 2 more pairs, on the same side on pin A_2; these will be the worker pairs for the edge.

Work in cloth stitch through the three passive pairs to pin-hole *A*. Twist the workers 3 times and place the pin. Work back in cloth stitch through the passive pairs to *B*, and twist the worker pair 3 times; place pin *B* (Figs 4e-g). This worker pair will work to the right. Its other end, anchored at A_2, will be the worker pair for the left-hand edge.

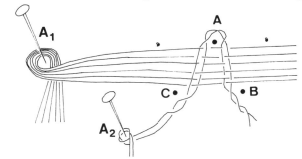

Fig 4e   *Setting in at pin-hole A to work in both directions*

Two pairs set in at pin *A* become worker pairs for the sides of the bookmark, one working the curved edge trail to the right, the other to the left.

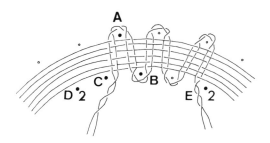

Fig 4f   *Working the curve to the right of pin A*

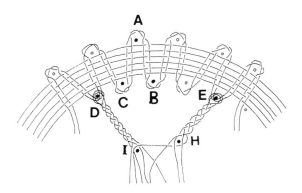

Fig 4g   *Working diagram for top of bookmark*

The plait pairs lead into the top pin-holes of the half-stitch bud. Note the threads of the first half-stitch between pin-holes H & I.

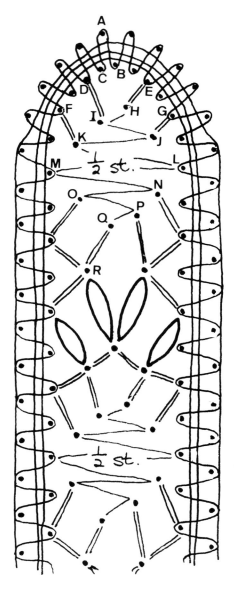

Fig 4h   *Working diagram for first half of bookmark* (prs)

Work in this way to pin-hole D and then to pin-hole E (Fig 4h). At each hang 2 pairs, from the back to the front of the pillow, to work the first two plaits.

Continue the edge to pin-holes F and G and hang in two more pairs at each for the 2 remaining plaits. You can now either carry on working the edge as a trail or change it to a footside.

To carry on, continue working the edges in cloth stitch, across the three passive pairs, twisting the workers 3 times before placing the pin, to form the winkie pins.

To change to a footside, start on the right-hand edge and work in cloth stitch through 2 pairs of passives; twist the worker pair twice and place the edge pin. Work a cloth stitch and twist both pairs twice. The left-hand pair becomes the worker pair, the right-hand pair the edge pair.

For the left-hand footside edge work in reverse order.

Work each side in your chosen way to the point where the edge will join the half-stitch bud, at pin-holes L & M. Make the four plaits before starting the half-stitch bud.

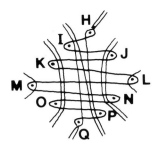

Fig 4i *Working the half-stitch bud*

The bud worker pair works a join with the worker pairs from the edges, first at pin-hole *L*, then at *M*. (prs)

Working the bud, Figs 4h & 4i Place pin *H* between the two pairs of the plait and work a half-stitch with the pairs. With the left-hand pair, work in half-stitch across the two pairs at pin-hole *I*; twist the worker pair once and place the pin. Work to pin-hole *J*; again, take in the plait pairs by working through the pairs in half-stitch and twisting the worker pair once, then place pin *J*. Work in the same way to pin-hole *L* where the two worker pairs from the bud and from the edge meet.

They can be joined in any of the following ways.

a. with a kiss stitch

b. by working a cloth stitch and one twist, placing the pin, then another cloth stitch and one twist

c. working a half-stitch, placing the pin, then another half-stitch.

For this exercise I chose method c.

Work pin-holes *L* & *M* in your chosen method. Continue working in half-stitch from pin *M* to *Q*, leaving out 2 pairs at each pin.

At pin *Q* there will be one pair left, and the worker pair itself. Work a half-stitch, place the pin and work a plait to the next pin-hole, *R*. Follow Fig 4h to continue. Work evenly down the pricking, making plaits and tallies as shown.

Note that pairs from plaits join the edge trail and leave immediately on the same side, as in Patterns 1 & 3.

Finishing, Figs 4c & 4d Follow either diagram to finish the bookmark.

Pl 4a *Enlarged top of bookmark*

Note detail of the beginning, the change from trail to footsides, and the large half-stitch buds.

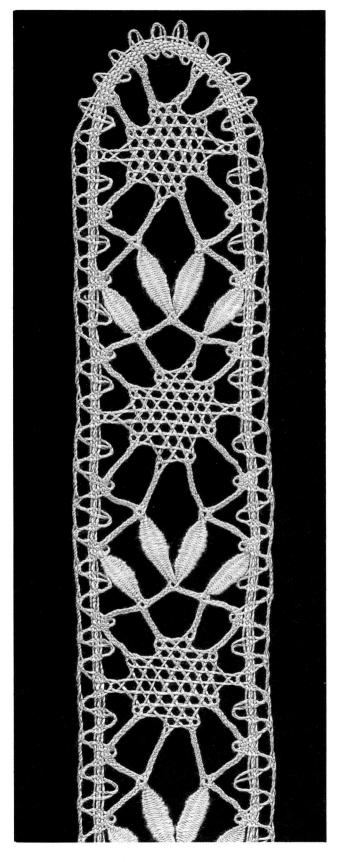

Pattern 5
Border with a deep scallop

This traditional pattern is probably of Cluny origin as suggested by the twisted headside. Its deep scallops and trail provide exercises in working a pointed join between scallop heads, and in using the trail as a convenient place to lay back unwanted pairs.

The design requires a way of working a corner different from that given in Pattern 2. In this case the added pairs are worked across the corner line and joined into the headside trail from which other pairs are removed to keep the number constant.

Introducing Decorating the headside edge with a twisted outer passive pair and winkie pins, two ways of working a pointed join between scalloped heads, another method of working a corner (see Pattern 2), adding pairs at the footside corner, working and joining them into the headside trail, and removing others from the headside.

Materials 12 pairs of bobbins + 2 pairs for the corner: Madeira Tanne 50, or Linen 120, or Retors d'Alsace 50.

Techniques

Using a twisted outer passive pair and winkie pins on the headside, Fig 5a To obtain a special effect at the headside edge twist the outer *passive* pair once between each row and work the winkie pins with four twists of the worker pair, as shown.

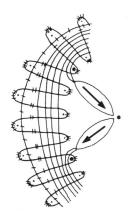

Fig 5a
Headside decorated with a twisted passive pair (prs)

Working a pointed join between scalloped heads, Fig 5b & 5c The scalloped headside with a trail is common in Bedfordshire patterns. The join between the heads is often pointed and a plait usually comes into the trail there. It needs special attention.

Work the headside trail to pin-hole *x* and leave the worker pair there to one side.

Turn to the inner point at *y* and work a crossing: work the two pairs from the plait in cloth stitch through the two right-hand passive pairs of the trail. The pairs will thereby have changed

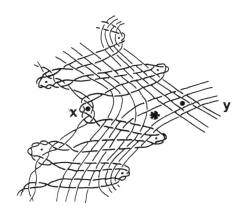

Fig 5b *Inner point of a scalloped headside*

The pin is placed in the centre of the join, at *y*, to create a deeper point.

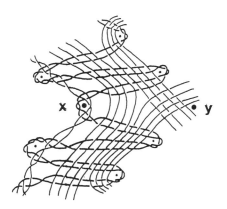

Fig 5c *Another way of working the inner point of a scalloped headside*

The pin is placed to the right of the join to tighten up the threads.

places: the two passive pairs from the trail will become the pairs for the next plait, and the pairs from the incoming plait will become part of the trail passives.

Pin y can be placed a. in the centre of the crossing (Fig 5b), or b. to the right of the crossing (Fig 5c).

Method a. will give a looser appearance and may create a small hole between the crossing and the trail, as shown in the sample (Pl 5a), which you may not like. To fill the hole, after completing the crossing work a cloth stitch (marked * in Fig 5b) with the right-hand pair from the trail and the left-hand pair from the crossing.

Method b. will give a tighter effect. Place the pin to the right of the completed crossing (Fig 5c).

Return to pin-hole x and continue working the headside.

Working the lace

Setting in and working the first head, Figs 5a & 5d-5e Start at the headside. Hang 2 sets of 2 pairs, straddled, over temporary pins above pin-hole A. With these pairs work a windmill crossing at A (Fig 5e). The two left-hand pairs will become passives in the headside trail and later be used to work a tally to F for the centre flower. The two right-hand pairs will first work as a plait to the footside and then work another flower tally to F.

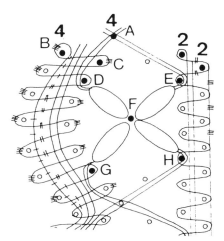

Fig 5d   *Start of working diagram* (prs)

Pl 5

Pl 5a   *Enlarged section of Pl 5*

The small hole in the clothwork of the inner scallop point occurs when Method *a* is used.

35

Hang 4 pairs on a temporary pin above pin-hole B: first 2 pairs side by side, for the trail passives, then 2 pairs, straddled, for the trail worker pair and the twisted edge pair. With the last 2 pairs work a half-stitch. Twist the outer (worker) pair 4 times and place pin B under it; this will form the outer twisted edge or winkie pin. Work a cloth stitch with the next pair and twist both pairs once. Continue to the right and work in cloth stitch, first through the two remaining pairs from the temporary pin above B, then across the two left-hand pairs from A. Twist the workers 3 times and place pin C. Carefully remove the temporary pins and ease the threads into position.

Work the headside trail for two more rows, to D, twisting the worker pair 4 times at the outer edge and once between the outer passive pair and the next pair in.

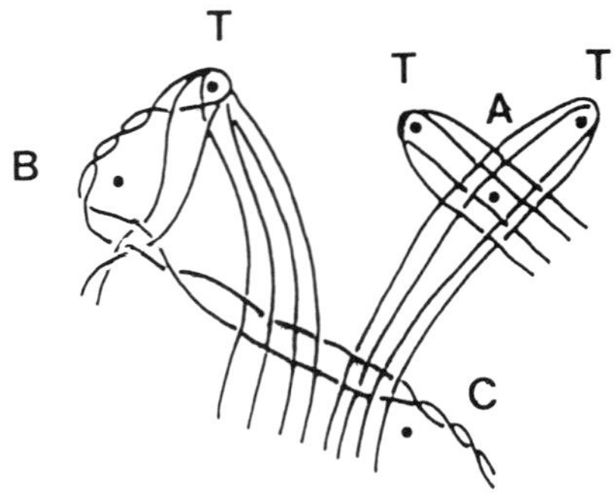

Fig 5e   *Setting in the headside*

Note the use of temporary pins to set in pairs at pin-holes A & B.

Fig 5d   *Working diagram* (prs)

Remember to twist the outer passive pair once between every row.

After placing pin D, leave out 2 pairs to work the tally to F.

Return to A (Fig 5d) and with the two pairs waiting there work a plait and left-hand picot to E.

Set in the footside. Follow Fig 5d and instructions for Pattern 1, Fig 1g. Hang 2 edge pairs straddled, and 2 pairs side by side, on a temporary pin for the passives.

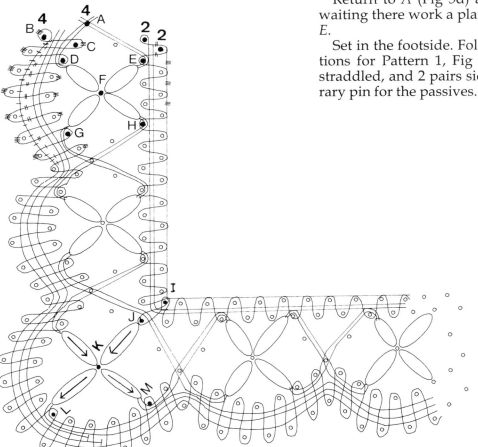

At pin-hole E, take in the plait pairs from A and leave them out immediately to make the tally to F. At F work a windmill crossing with the tally pairs from D & E and then work the tallies to G & H to form the 4-petal flower.

Work the headside to pin-hole G. Between pins D & G the trail will be short of 2 pairs used to work the tally to F. To fill the space in this section, twist the worker pair twice between the outer passive pair and the next one in (Fig 5a).

At G take in the tally pairs and revert to one twist of the workers until two pairs leave the trail at the next head to make another tally.

Continue working the footside, taking in the tally pairs at pin-hole H and leaving them out again to work a plait (with a left-hand picot) towards the inner point of the scalloped trail. Follow Figs 5b&c and instructions to work the pointed join between the scalloped heads.

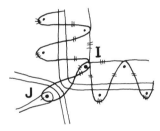

Fig 5f   *Working the inner corner*

Detail for pin-holes I to J. Pin-hole I is worked twice.

At pin-hole J the footside worker works twice through the incoming plait pairs; they leave immediately to form the ground for the next side. Also at J two pairs are added to work the tally to K. (prs)

Working the corner, Figs 5d, 5f-5g Two extra pairs (hung on at J) will be needed to work the corner, and pin-hole I will be worked twice.

Work the lace to pin-holes I & L. At I, work to the left, through two footside passive pairs and through the plait pairs at J. Hang 2 pairs, from the back to the front of the pillow, to the right of pin-hole J. Work through the added pairs, twist once and place pin J. Work back to corner pin I; remove it and replace it under the worker pair. Untwist the outer pair, work a cloth stitch, and re-twist the outer pair 3 times and the inner pair twice. The inner pair will be the worker pair for the next footside.

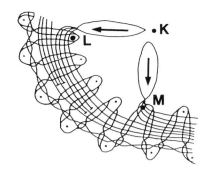

Fig 5g   *Removing pairs from the outer corner trail*

Although the blocked lines indicate removed pairs, it is in fact *alternate* threads which are laid to the back of the pillow, to avoid holes in the fabric.

Bring the ends of the new pairs at J together and work a tally to K, a windmill crossing at K with the pairs from the incoming tally, and another tally to L. Turn the pillow.

At pin-hole L, Fig 5g, take the tally pairs into the trail and lay existing pairs from the trail to the back of the pillow, to make room for the incoming pairs and to keep the number of pairs constant.

Figure 5d shows pairs being removed; remember that in fact you need to take out threads, one at a time, from alternate pairs, as shown in Fig 5g.

Finishing To finish the border follow instructions for Pattern 1.

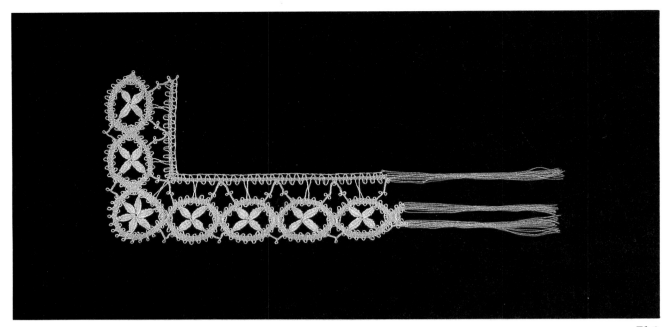

Pl 6

Pattern 6
Border with crossing trails

This old Bedfordshire pattern provides a lesson in crossing trails, a common feature in traditional designs.

We shall cover two techniques, either of which is suitable for this pattern. The first applies to trails of equal width crossing at an angle like the one in this border. The second can be used not only here but also for trails of different widths and crossing at the various angles found in older prickings.

Also shown in this pattern are another method of joining a plait to a trail and two ways of decorating headside scallops in the same pricking.

Introducing Crossing trails of equal or different widths at different angles, joining plait pairs to a trail to stay in the trail for several rows, using winkie pins and a picot to decorate a scalloped headside.

Materials 18 pairs of bobbins + 4 pairs for the corner: Madeira Tanne 50, or Retors d'Alsace 50, or Linen 120.

Techniques

Crossing trails of equal width at a specific angle, Fig 6a This technique is used when trails of equal width cross at approximately the angle shown in the diagram.

Work each trail as far as the joint pin-hole *a*. Twist the worker pairs once. Work a cloth stitch with the worker pairs, twist both pairs once and place pin *a*. Work another cloth stitch. Work each pair back through the passives of its own side to *b* & *c*; twist 3 times, place the pins and leave to one side.

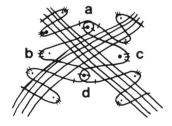

Fig 6a   *Crossing of trails at a 90° angle* (prs)

38

Starting at the centre, work each of the passives in the left-hand trail through the passives of the right-hand trail in cloth stitch. All pairs will have changed place. Pull up all passives firmly.

With each worker pair work in cloth stitch from its own side to the centre, to join at centre pin-hole *d*. Work them together in cloth stitch, twist both pairs once, place pin *d*, work another cloth stitch, and twist both pairs once again.

Continue the trails separately.

Crossing trails of different widths at various angles, Fig 6b Work each trail as far as the joint pin-hole *e*. Twist both worker pairs once. Work a cloth stitch with the worker pairs, twist both pairs once, and place pin *e*. Work another cloth stitch. One of the worker pairs now becomes a passive pair. With the other pair work in cloth stitch back through its own side to *f*, twist 3 times and place pin *f*.

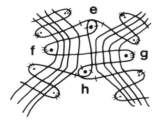

Fig 6b   *Crossing trails of different widths at different angles*

This older method is more versatile than the one in Fig 6a, but the crossing may sometimes end up with too many or too few pairs. (prs)

Work in cloth stitch across all the passive pairs to *g*, twist the workers 3 times, and place pin *g*. Work back in cloth stitch through half the passive pairs *and* the ex-worker pair, which now becomes a worker again. Twist both pairs once, place pin *h*, work a cloth stitch and twist both pairs once. Use these two worker pairs to continue working their respective trails, as shown.

Joining a plait to a trail to stay for several rows, Fig 6c & 6d With the worker pair work in cloth stitch across the passives and the plait pairs.

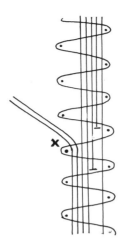

Fig 6c   *Joining and removing plait pairs from a trail*

Pairs are removed before new ones join the trail at *x*, which keeps the number even. Note the staggered removal of the pairs; see also Fig 6d. (prs)

Twist the workers twice, place pin *x* and continue working.

If the plait pairs are likely to make the trail too bulky, lay back two threads from the row before taking in the plait, and another two threads in the row after taking it in. Fig 6d shows the position where the threads should be taken out.

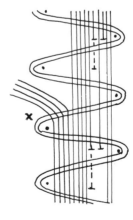

Fig 6d   *Detail of Fig 6c*

Dotted lines show how the removal of surplus pairs can be staggered even further to avoid holes in the lace.

Working the lace

Setting in and working the first head, Figs 6e & 6f
Start at the headside and hang pairs as shown: 2 pairs side by side on a temporary pin above pin-hole *E*, and 2 sets of 4 pairs each side by side on temporary pins above the trails.

Hang 2 pairs, straddled, on a pin at *A*, and twist twice (see Fig 6e). Work a cloth stitch with them. These are the worker pairs for the trails. With the left-hand pair work in cloth stitch through the left-hand set of 4 passive pairs. With the right-hand pair work through the right-hand set of 4 passive pairs. Twist each worker pair four times, place pins *B* & *C* and leave the workers to one side.

With each pair of the left-hand trail in turn, work in cloth stitch through the pairs of the right-hand trail.

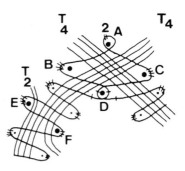

Fig 6e *Setting in the headside trails* (prs)

Remove the temporary pins and pull all pairs down firmly.

Return to the worker pairs at *B* & *C* and work each in cloth stitch through the passive pairs on their side, to pin-hole *D*. With the two pairs work a cloth stitch, twist once, and place the pin; work another cloth stitch and twist once.

Work the left-hand trail to pin-hole *E*, taking in the two pairs hanging from the temporary pin above it. Work in cloth stitch to pin-hole *F* and leave out two pairs for a tally.

Return to the right-hand trail and work to pin-hole *G*; leave out two pairs here for another tally.

Set in the footside, as for Pattern 1, Fig 1g. Hang 2 pairs on a temporary pin for the passives, 2 pairs as edge pair and worker pair, and 2 extra pairs at pin-hole *H* (Fig 6f) which will be left out immediately for the plait.

With the two pairs left out at *H* make a plait with double picots to reach the trail at pin-hole *I*.

Return to pin-hole *G*. Work across the trail and take in the pairs from the plait at pin-hole *I*.

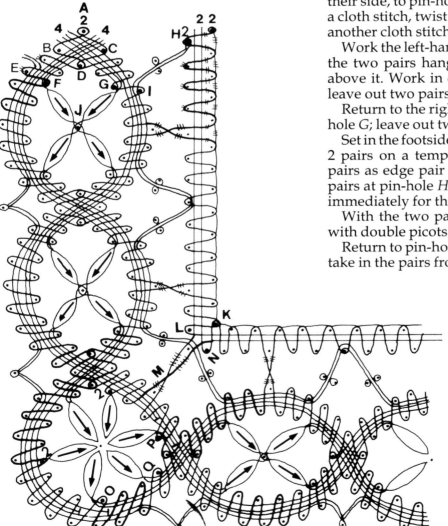

Fig 6f *Working diagram* (prs)

Two ways of decorating the outer edge of a headside: with picots, or by workers well twisted round a *winkie pin*.

Now work the tallies from *F* & *G* to pin-hole *J* while there is enough room to do so. Work a windmill crossing for the flower centre, and make the two remaining tallies. While the tallies are waiting to be taken into the trails, hang their worker threads over conveniently placed pins, to ensure they retain their shape. Work the right-hand trail, joining it to the footside with a kiss stitch.

At the headside, between the heads, leave out 2 pairs and make a plait with a left-hand picot, as shown.

Note how the design ensures the number of pairs in the trail remains constant: 2 pairs from the tally join the trail, and 2 other pairs leave to work the plait with a picot.

Work the lace down to the corner at *K*.

Working the corner, Figs 6f & 6g   Four extra pairs are needed to work the six tallies for the corner flower. Follow Fig 6f and add the two sets of 2 pairs, laying them from the back to the front of the pillow, at the pin-holes shown. Work the first three tallies, whose arrows point to the centre of the flower, then the six-pair crossing (Pattern 2, Fig 2d), and return to the inner corner.

Follow Fig 6g and work through the footside pairs, from pin *K* to pin-hole *L*. Place pin *L*. Work back in cloth stitch through two passive pairs and leave the worker pair as a passive for the next footside. Next, use the first passive pair worked through after pin *L* as the worker pair, and work to the left through the incoming plait pairs.

Twist the worker 3 to 5 times as shown, and work a kiss stitch at *M* with the worker pair from the inner trail. Having worked the kiss stitch, use the right-hand pair and work through the plait pairs again and through one footside passive pair. Leave this worker pair to become a passive pair for the next footside. Twist the passive pair just worked through 3 times; place pin *N* under it. Work in cloth stitch to the right through the two new passive pairs; twist twice. Remove pin *K* and re-pin under the worker pair. Take the twists off the edge pair and work a cloth stitch with the worker pair; twist twice and continue with the next footside.

Work the second half of the corner flower and take the pairs from the tallies into the trails at *O*, *P* & *Q*. Lay back 2 pairs from each trail before the next trail crossing, as shown.

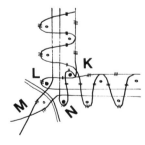

Fig 6g   *Working the inner corner*

The first footside passive pair, from *L*, works through the incoming plait pairs and makes a kiss stitch at *M* with the worker pairs from the inner trail. Corner pin-hole *K* is worked twice. (prs)

Finishing   To join the completed edging, follow instructions for Pattern 1.

41

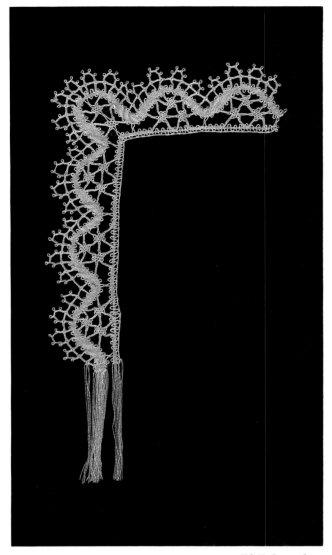

Pl 7 *Sample a*

Pl 7a *Sample b*

Pattern 7

Square border with 'spider' ground

This pattern, typical of old Bedfordshire designs with its scalloped trail and *spider* ground, has been adapted from a pricking in the collection of Luton Museum. It provides an exercise in the technique of Bedfordshire *spider* or *bud* ground, and together with the next three patterns forms a sampler of grounds commonly found in Bedfordshire lace. These can be joined to make a cover for a ring cushion, see Fig 10f & Pl 10b.

The two samples illustrate the problem of bulky trails that can form in Bedfordshire patterns and show how the lace-maker can overcome it by removing threads. Sample a. shows the bulky effect of leaving all the threads in the trail, while sample b. has been improved by laying back 2 pairs (4 threads); though in this case 2 new pairs will have to be added to work the first plait in the next head.

Introducing The Bedfordshire spider or bud ground, removing threads from a trail to avoid bulkiness.

42

Materials 20 pairs of bobbins: Madeira Tanne 50, or DMC Fil à Broder machine 50.

Techniques

Bedfordshire spider or bud ground, Fig 7a The ground is composed of buds or 'spider' motifs linked by plaits. The bud is worked the same way as in Pattern 4, in rows of half-stitch. Pairs from three plaits are fed into the bud, work half-way down the bud and are taken out again either to feed into other buds or to join other parts of the pattern.

Follow Fig 7a. Work the plaits to pin-holes *a, b* & *c*; place the top pin between the plait pairs at *a*; work a half-stitch with the pairs to enclose the pin.

From *a* work in half-stitch towards *b*, the next highest pin-hole on the pattern, using the pair nearest to it as the worker, in this case the left-hand pair at *a*. Work across the plait pairs at *b*; twist the workers once and place the pin.

Work in half-stitch to *c*, taking in the plait pairs. Twist the workers once, and place pin *c*. Continue in half-stitch, twisting the workers once at the pins, and leaving out 2 pairs at a time, at *d, e* & *f*. The pairs from these pins will be plaited to the next part of the ground as indicated in the pattern and Figs 7c&d.

Removing or laying back pairs, Fig 7b The trail can accommodate (within limits) a varying number of threads. If there are too few, the eye will no longer recognise it as a trail and the design may be lost. If there are too many, they may create an unsightly bumpiness. The technique of removing and adding pairs will help the lace-maker maintain the right balance.

Lay back pairs which have been in the trail longest so that they are well anchored in the fabric before being cut off. Never remove threads lying side by side, nor an edge thread. Take out threads on the opposite side to where new pairs are being added (Fig 7b).

Cut off threads singly when the lace is clear of pins. Take one at a time and run a small, sharp pair of scissors down it close to the work; snip it off *very* carefully.

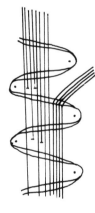

Fig 7b   *Removing pairs from the trail*

Pairs need removing or the trail becomes too thick. They will need replacing in the next head.

Working the lace

You will need to work six heads to obtain the square border required for the ring cushion cover, though this would not be large enough for a handkerchief. One extra head has been included on the pricking to allow for the setting up (lifting) of the lace.

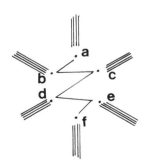

Fig 7a
Bedfordshire spider (prs/thr)

43

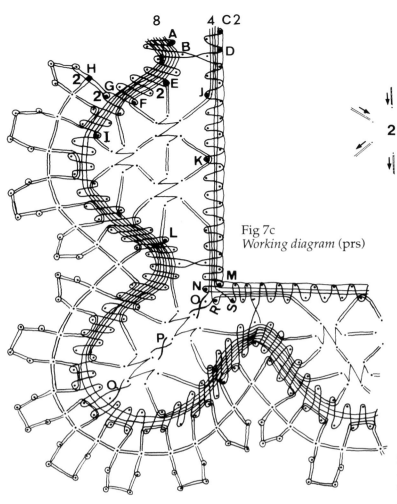

8   4 C 2
A
B
  D
H
2   G   E
2   2   J
F
I

K

L

M
N
O R S
P

Q

Fig 7c
Working diagram (prs)

Fig 7d
Working the three spiders in order

The arrows show how plait pairs lead into the spider buds and out again. (prs)

1
2
3

Setting in and working the first head, Fig 7c
Begin with the trail. Hang 8 pairs side by side on a temporary pin above pin-hole A. Take the first pair on the left as the worker pair and work in cloth stitch to the right, through the other seven pairs; place pin A. Work to the 3rd pin, B, twist the worker pair 3 times and leave to one side (in readiness for the kiss stitch).

Set in the footside. Hang in 4 pairs side by side on a temporary pin above C (for the footside passives), and 2 pairs straddled on pin C itself (the edge pairs).

There will be 4 pairs of passives in the footside up to pin-hole J where 2 pairs will leave to work a plait for the spider ground.

Work the footside to pin D, then work a kiss stitch with the trail worker waiting at pin-hole B.

Return to the trail. Hang in 2 pairs at pin-hole E, and work the top plait for the spider ground. Continue to pin-hole F where 2 pairs will leave the trail to work another plait for the spider

ground. Work another row, and add 2 more pairs at pin-hole G, for the ninepin edge.

To start the ninepin edge work a plait to H; at H add 2 pairs (for the ninepin bar) and work a windmill crossing. Note the varying width of the ninepin.

Continue the ninepin and the trail until the 4th plait leaves the trail at I for the spider ground.

Return to the footside. Work to pin-hole J and leave 2 pairs to work another plait for the spider ground.

Working the spider ground, Figs 7c & 7d   The arrows in Fig 7d show the order in which the spiders are to be worked. After completing Spider 1, work the footside to pin-hole K, to allow you to take in the lower right-hand plait from the spider and immediately leave it out again for Spider 3.

Work Spiders 2 & 3, leaving the worked plaits ready for taking into the headside and footside as work progresses.

Return to the trail and the headside. Follow Fig 7c and work to pin-hole L. At L lay back from the trail one pair just before taking into it the last plait from Spider 3, and another pair just after. Remember to remove pairs as single threads, not lying next to each other (Fig 7b). Replace these pairs with new pairs at the next head, where the plait pairs leave the trail to work Spider 1.

Working the corner, Figs 7c & 7e   No new pairs will be needed to work the corner because the corner line will be formed by kiss stitches. However, while working the corner you will need to turn the pillow backwards and forwards a little so that the lace always faces you.

Work the lace up to a line defined by pin-holes O, P & Q. Note that the corner ground is made up of 2 spiders. At Q twist the trail worker pair 3 times in readiness for the kiss stitch. Work the

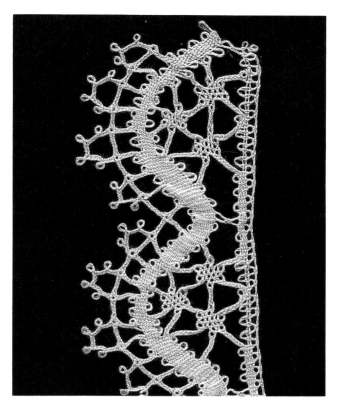

Pl 7b *Sample a*

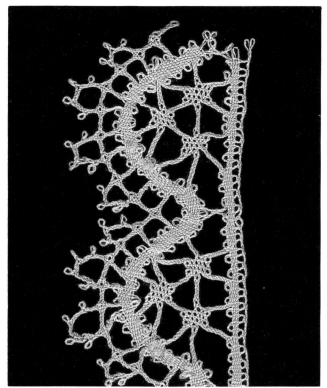

Pl 7c *Sample b*

Pl 7b&c   *Two methods of working the trail*

In *a* all the pairs remain in the trail. In *b* two pairs are removed and two added in the next head.

outer spider to its 3rd pin and twist the worker pair 3 times in readiness for the kiss stitch at *P*. Work the inner spider also to its 3rd pin; twist the worker pair 3 times in readiness for the kiss stitch at *O*, to be made with the worker pair from the footside.

Having worked pin *M* (Fig 7e), work another footside row and place pin *N*. Work back through 3 passives and leave the worker pair as a passive pair for the next footside.

Take the first passive pair at *N* as a worker pair, twist 3 times and work the kiss stitch at *O* with the worker pair from the inner spider. Now work to the 4th pin-hole of the inner spider, twist the worker 3 times and work a kiss stitch at *P* with the worker from the outer spider. Work across the spider to its 4th pin; twist the workers 3 times and work a kiss stitch at *Q* with the trail worker pair waiting there.

Complete the spiders. Turn the pillow a little and return to the inner corner. You used the first footside passive pair for the kiss stitch, so now

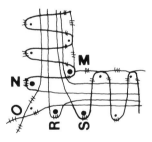

Fig 7e   *Working the inner corner* (prs)

with the second footside passive pair work through the incoming kiss stitch pair, and place pin *R*. Work through two pairs and leave it as a passive pair for the next side. The last pair worked through now becomes the worker pair, working across one pair to the left. Place pin *S*.

Continue working down the pricking.

Finishing   To join the beginning and end of the edging, follow instructions in Pattern 1. Fig 10f shows how to assemble the pieces of lace for the ring cushion.

45

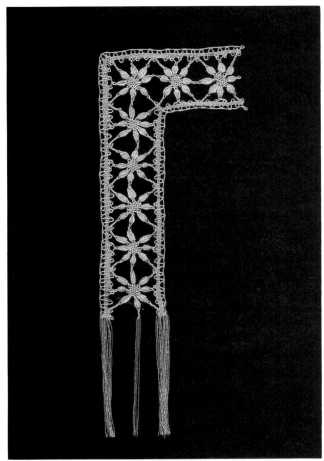

PI 8

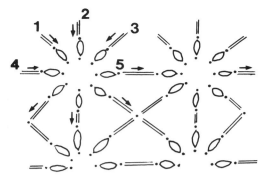

Fig 8a *Flower ground*

The tallies should be rounded so that they stand out against the joining plaits. The centre is worked in half-stitch like a bud or a spider. (prs)

Techniques

Flower ground, Fig 8a As well as being used to form a ground, the motif can be used in a single row, as in this pattern. The flowers are made up of tallies with a half-stitch bud in the centre, and plaits joining into the other parts of the pattern. The tallies should be as rounded as possible to differentiate them from the joining plaits.

The arrows and numbers in Fig 8a indicate the order of working the plaits and tallies, and the taking in and out of pairs. The horizontal row of tallies and plaits is shown worked from left to right, but this order can be reversed, depending on the position of the incoming pairs.

Follow Fig 8a, which shows a ground of two flowers next to each other, joined by a horizontal plait.

Start by working the top 3 tallies of the flowers. Next, assuming you are working from left to right, work the tally on the extreme left of the ground (No 4). If you are working in the other direction work the tally on the extreme right (No 5).

Work the upper part of the half-stitch buds to their 4th pin-hole and take in the pairs from Tally 4. Work across the half-stitch bud of the first flower, to the 5th pin-hole, and leave out 2 pairs to form Tally 5. Work Tally 5, place the pin, work the joining plait and then the horizontal tally for the next flower.

Work across the half-stitch bud of the next flower in the same way as you did the first. The horizontal plait, shown by the arrow, will join another flower, or another part of the pattern.

Work the lower part of the half-stitch buds and the tallies, leaving out pairs for the joining plaits, as shown by the arrows.

Pattern 8

Square insertion with Bedfordshire flower ground

The flower ground shown in this pattern is often found in the more elaborate lace designs created between about 1850 and 1890. Here, used on its own, it has a distinctly modern look.

When the pattern is used for the ring cushion seven flower heads and a corner head need to be worked on each side. An extra head has been drawn on the pricking to allow for the setting up (lifting) of the lace. Both edges will be worked as footsides.

Introducing Bedfordshire flower ground.

Materials 16 pairs of bobbins + 2 pairs for the corner: Madeira Tanne 50, or DMC Fil à Broder machine 50.

46

Working the lace

Setting in and working the first head, Fig 8b Set in both footsides at the same time. Hang 2 pairs on each of the first footside pins, *A & B*; hang 6 pairs side by side on a temporary pin above *A*, and 4 pairs side by side on a temporary pin above pin *B*, as shown.

Start at the outer footside, pin *A*. With the two pairs work a cloth stitch and twist both pairs twice. With the right-hand pair work in cloth stitch through the six passive pairs, place the pin, and twist three times; work back in cloth stitch through 6 passive pairs, and leave out two pairs for the first plait and Tally 2. Continue with the outer footside until you have placed 6 pins. At this pin leave out one pair and at the 8th pin leave out another pair. Twist both pairs 3 times; work together in cloth stitch, twist once, place the pin and leave aside for Tally 4 (see Fig 8c).

Return to the inner footside, Fig 8b. With the two pairs at pin *B* work a cloth stitch, and twist twice. With the left-hand pair work to the left, through the four pairs of passives; leave out 2 pairs for the plait and Tally 3. Continue working the footside to the 6th pin-hole and leave aside.

Working the flower ground Hang 2 pairs, straddled, at pin *C* and make Tally 1.

With the two pairs left out at the 2nd pin of the outer footside, work the plait to Tally 2; place the pin between the pairs and make Tally 2. With the pairs left out at the 2nd pin of the inner footside, work a plait to Tally 3; place the pin between the pairs and make Tally 3.

Make Tally 4.

Working the flower centre, Fig 8c Start the half-stitch centre like any other bud (see Pattern 4, Fig 4b & Pattern 7, Fig 7a). Place a pin between the pairs at the end of Tally 1. Work in half-stitch to the left, taking in the pairs from Tally 2; twist the worker pair once, place the pin.

Work in half-stitch to the right, taking in the pairs from Tally 3; twist the worker pair once, place the pin.

Work in half-stitch to the left, taking in the pairs from Tally 4; twist the worker pair once, place the pin.

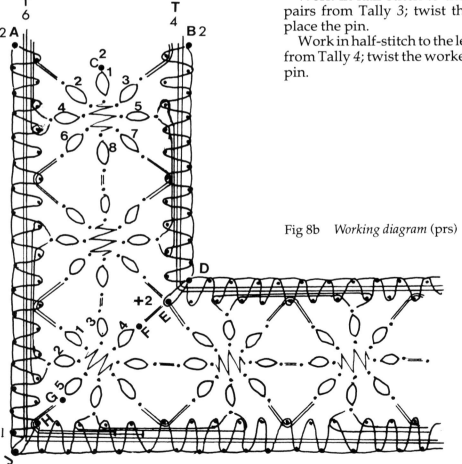

Fig 8b   *Working diagram* (prs)

47

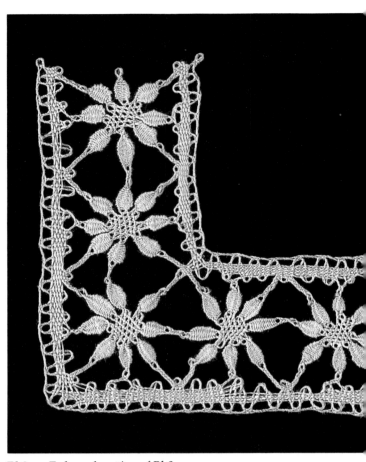

Fig 8c *Working the flower head*

The numbers show the order of working the pointed tallies. The arrows show the passage of the pairs from one side of the pattern to the other, changing direction in each head. (prs)

Work in half-stitch to the right, across 7 passive pairs; place the pin, twist once; leave out two pairs for Tally 5.

Work to the left in the same way, leaving out pairs for Tallies 6, 7, & 8.

Work Tally 5, place the pin, work a cloth stitch and twist each pair three times. Take the pairs into the footside at two separate pin-holes, as shown in Figs 8b & 8c. They will remain in the footside as passive pairs until the next flower, where they will be left out at separate pin-holes ready to work the horizontal tallies across the half-stitch bud to the *left*, as shown by the arrows. This horizontal working will continue from bud to bud moving alternately to the left and to the right.

Complete the first half-stitch bud with Tallies 6, 7 & 8; continue the footsides and start the next flower.

Pl 8a *Enlarged section of Pl 8*

In one head the horizontal pairs work from one side of the flower to the other. In the next they work in the opposite direction. See also Fig 8c.

***Working the corner**, Figs 8b, 8d & 8e* The tallies of the corner flower will be worked in a different order and are numbered in the order of working.

Work to the corner flower, making Tallies 1, 2 & 3. After working the inner footside pin D (Fig 8d), work to pin-hole E, across the two footside passive pairs and the two plait pairs from the previous flower. At pin E add 2 extra pairs (laying them from back to the front of the pillow) to work the corner flower.

Work back in cloth stitch from pin E to pin D through the pairs taken in at E and the two footside passives. Twist twice and re-work pin D.

Return to the two extra pairs at E, make a plait to F and Tally 4.

Work the half-stitch bud.

Work Tally 5 to pin-hole G (Fig 8e) and then a plait to the corner pin-hole H. Take the two plait pairs into the outer footside trail and lay them back after a few rows, as shown.

48

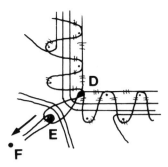

Fig 8d   *Working the inner corner*

Two pairs are added at pin-hole E for the corner flower. Pin-hole *D* is worked twice. (prs)

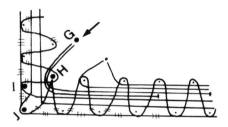

Fig 8e   *Detail of outer corner* (prs)

After you have worked pin-hole *H*, work one more footside row to pin-hole *I*. Work back through two pairs of passives and leave the worker pair as a passive pair for the next side (Fig 8e).

Now take the outer passive pair, *not the edge pair itself*, as the worker pair for the outer corner pin-hole *J* and for the next side. Twist the new worker pair twice, place pin *J*, work a cloth stitch, and twist the edge pair twice. Turn the pillow. Work in cloth stitch through the 4 pairs to pin *H*; re-work pin *H* and continue working down the next side.

Finishing   To finish the insertion follow instructions for Pattern 1, Fig 1i.

Pattern 9

Square insertion with plaited ground

The pattern is an exercise in Bedfordshire plaited ground. The technique is often found in early Bedfordshire lace designs of the 1850s and 1860s, and was taken from Honiton lace where it is called *diamond filling*. It is made up of square-ended tallies and used here as the main feature in an insertion.

Since the regular dimensions of the ground don't quite match those of the square insertion to be worked on it, the corner design comes out the same on opposite sides but different on adjacent ones.

Note the double outer edge, joined by kiss stitches worked with only one support pin.

The pricking is small enough to be completed in a single operation, without having to be set up.

Introducing The square-ended tally and plaited ground, joining a plaited ground to a trail or footside, working corners with two different layouts of plaited ground, joining a double edge with kiss stitches.

Materials 14 pairs of bobbins + 2 pairs for the 2nd and 4th corners: Madeira Tanne 50, or DMC Fil à Broder machine 50.

Techniques

The square-ended tally, Fig 9a Like the pointed tally, the square-ended tally is a small block of weaving. It is made using two pairs which leave the clothwork at separate pin-holes.

Twist each pair three times; place the pin. The tally pins are used as markers, and to keep the pairs apart. Use the second thread from the left as the weaver, and weave over and under towards the right, then back again to the left over and under, and so on. To achieve the required rectangular shape hold the outer threads taut and the weaver loose. Finish with the weaver thread on the opposite side from the start, as shown. When the tally is long enough place the second marker pin and twist the pairs three times.

To retain the square-ended shape of the tally when you continue working, use **first** the pair **not** containing the weaver thread, shown on the bottom left of Fig 9a.

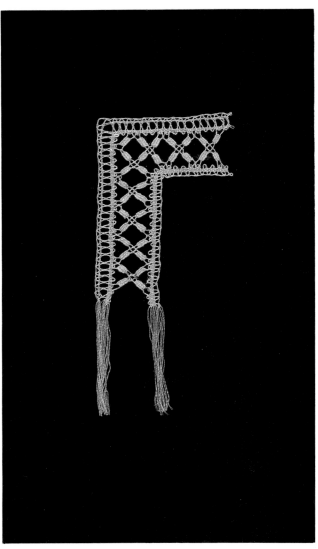

Pl 9

Fig 9a *Square ended tally*

The pins are used only as markers and the space between them should be filled. The width of the tally will depend on the initial space between the pairs. To continue, first use the pair *without* the weaver thread to avoid pulling the tally out of shape.

50

The plaited ground, Fig 9b A plaited ground is formed by crossings of square-ended tallies.

Make tallies *a* & *b*, taking the weaver thread marked * from the inner side of each. Work with each weaver thread to the opposite side, filling the space between the marker pin-holes. Leave the weaver threads aside over a pin. Place marker pins *c* & *d*.

Crossing *1*. Twist the inner pairs three times, pulling firmly in the direction they will work next, i.e. towards crossings *2* & *3*. Work a cloth stitch and twist three times. It is most important to pull the pairs firmly at this point as this will set the bottom of the tally squarely.

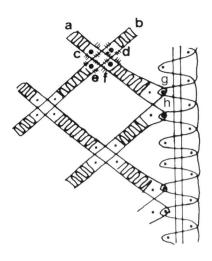

Fig 9c   *Plaited ground joined to the footside* (prs)

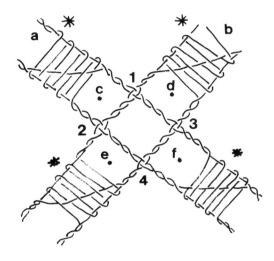

Fig 9b   *Plaited ground*

The pair to be worked first after a tally must not contain the weaver thread (see Fig 9a). Asterisks indicate the side from which the weaver thread was taken; after working the tally the weaver thread was left on the opposite side so that Crossing *1* did not contain one.

Crossings *2* & *3*. First take the pairs containing the weaver threads, which you have left aside, off the pins. Gently twist them three times. Work a cloth stitch at each crossing and twist the pairs three times.

Crossing *4*. Work a cloth stitch; twist each pair three times. Place marker pins *e* & *f* to start the next two tallies.

Before starting the next set of tallies consider the position of the next crossings and take the new weaver threads from the appropriate pairs; in this case from the outer pairs at *2* & *3*.

Joining the plaited ground to the footside, Fig 9c
Work a tally from *f*. Twist each pair three times; place the marker pin at the end of the tally. With the right-hand pair from the tally and the footside worker pair, work a cloth stitch, twist once, place pin *g*, and work a cloth stitch to enclose the pin. Twist the tally pair three times and work a cloth stitch with the left-hand pair from the tally. Twist both pairs three times. Work two rows of the footside. With the right-hand pair and the footside worker, work a cloth stitch, twist once, place pin *h*, and work another cloth stitch. Twist the tally pair three times; place the marker pin to start the next tally.

Working the lace

Setting in and working the first head, Fig 9d
Start at the headside and note the number of pairs. Work the two pairs at *B* together in cloth stitch; twist the right-hand pair three times and leave aside. Twist the left-hand pair once and work to the left in cloth stitch, across the three pairs of passives; twist three times in readiness for the kiss stitch.

Hang 3 pairs straddled on pin *A*. With the two left-hand pairs at *A* work a cloth stitch, twist twice. With the right-hand pair as the worker pair, work a cloth stitch to the right, through one pair of passives; twist the worker pair three times.

51

Make a kiss stitch with the worker pair from the second edge trail, place the support pin. Work to pin-hole B_1; twist the right-hand pair three times and leave out.

Use the two pairs left out at pin-holes B & B_1 to begin the plaited ground from the headside.

Turn to the footside. Hang 2 pairs straddled on pin C, and 4 pairs side by side on a temporary pin above C. With the two pairs at C work a cloth stitch, twist both pairs twice. With the left-hand pair work to the left in cloth stitch, across 4 pairs of passives. Leave out one pair at each of pin-holes C_1 & C_2 to work the ground as you did at the headside.

Work the plaited ground; see above (Fig 9b). Follow instructions for joining the ground to the footside given above (Fig 9c). To join the plaited ground to the headside work in reverse order.

Work to the first corner pin-hole, D.

Note that the two sets of facing corners differ from each other. In one set the right-hand diagonal of the tallies falls on either side of the corner line (Fig 9d) while in the other they fit the corner line exactly (Fig 9e).

Fig 9d *Working diagram*

Setting in and working the first set of corners. (prs)

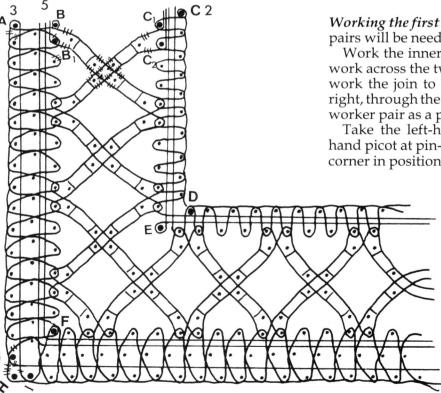

Pl 9a *Enlarged first corner of Pl 9*

The second corner is slightly different but can be worked from the detailed diagram, Fig 9e.

Working the first set of corners, Fig 9d No extra pairs will be needed to work the corner.

Work the inner corner: having worked pin D, work across the two pairs of footside passives to work the join to the ground. Work back to the right, through the footside passives, and leave the worker pair as a passive for the next side.

Take the left-hand passive and make a left-hand picot at pin-hole E. This will hold the inner corner in position neatly.

Work a cloth stitch to the right, through one pair of passives, and leave as a passive for the next side. The passive pair just worked through will now become the worker pair for the next side.

Work the outer corner: Work the plaited ground and the headside trails to pin-hole F. After placing pin F, work across the two inner trail passives. Work a kiss stitch with the worker from the outer edge trail. Continue by working a cloth stitch to the right, through the first passive pair of the inner trail, then leave it to become a passive pair for the next side.

Return to the kiss stitch. With the worker pair that came from pin-hole F work in cloth stitch through the passive pair of the outer edge trail, twist the worker twice, place pin G. Work a cloth stitch with the outer edge pair, and twist the pairs twice. With the right-hand pair work a cloth stitch with the outer passive pair and leave it as a passive pair for the next side.

Twist the outer edge pair from pin G four times, place pin H and turn the pillow. After placing pin H work the two outer pairs in cloth stitch, twist twice, and place pin I on the inside.

With the right-hand pair at I work in cloth stitch to the right, through the passive pair, and twist three times. Work the kiss stitch with the first pair lying to the right, which is the first passive pair in the inner edge trail.

Work in cloth stitch through the next two pairs to the right; re-work pin F.

Working the second set of corners, Fig 9e Add 2 pairs at pin-hole J. Twist one of the pairs 3 or 4 times to reach pin-hole K, and twist the other three times so that the pairs are separated before starting the square-ended tally.

Now work the outer corner. From pin J work through two passive pairs, and work a kiss stitch. Continue working the inner and outer corner pin-holes as for the previous corner, following instructions for pin-holes F, G, H & I, Fig 9d. After working pin-hole H turn the pillow, then work to pin-hole I. Work the new side to pin K where the left-hand twisted pair from J is taken into the work and immediately left out for the tally. Twist this pair three times and use it together with the pair from J to make the corner line of tallies.

Work the tallies on the diagonal corner line as indicated by the arrows, from pin-holes J & K to the inner corner pin-holes L & M.

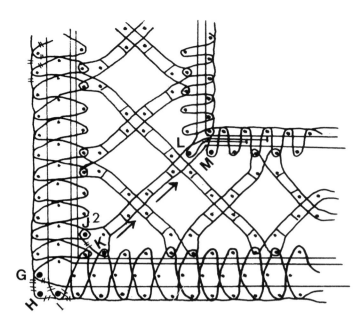

Fig 9e *Working the second set of corners* (prs)

At L take into the corner the first of the two added pairs, by working through it with the inner passive of the footside pairs. Take the second pair into the footside at pin-hole M with the footside worker from the inner corner.

Remove two pairs from the footside by laying them back several rows after the corner, as shown.

Finishing To join the beginning and end of the insertion follow instructions in Pattern 1, Fig 1i.

When completed the square insertion will fit inside the lace of Pattern 8, though it can also be used as a frame or a border.

Pattern 10

Square insertion with Bedfordshire ground

This pattern shows how a modern look can be achieved with the common Bedfordshire ground. It completes the ring cushion set.

The design is made up of plaits, with and without picots, framed by a trail. The picots can be right-hand, left-hand, or double. At the very centre of the piece are 2 double picots worked very closely on either side of a windmill crossing. This is the basic unit of the Bedfordshire version of Honiton blossom filling.

The preceding four patterns were intended to introduce new techniques, step by step. In this new pattern the lace-maker can take advantage of its simple ground to improvise, and make up individual designs of picots. The pattern can also be used on its own, for a brooch or in any other frame.

Introducing Bedfordshire blossom ground, removing a large number of pairs from a trail.

Materials 40 pairs of bobbins: Madeira Tanne 50, or DMC Fil à Broder machine 50.

Techniques

Bedfordshire blossom ground, Fig 10a   This is an adaptation by Bedfordshire lace-makers of the Honiton blossom filling. The four picots are worked in the order shown by the lettering, with a windmill crossing in the centre marked by a pin-hole.

Make the right-hand plait long enough to reach pin-hole *a*. Make a left-hand picot at *a*; work a half-stitch with the two pairs and make a right-hand picot at *b*. Work a half-stitch with the two pairs.

Fig 10a   *Blossom ground*

A Bedfordshire method of working the Honiton Blossom filling. (prs)

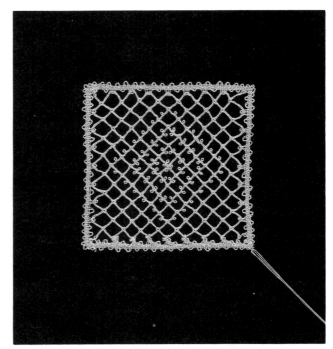

Work a windmill crossing with the plaits at the centre pin-hole; with the left-hand (formerly the right-hand) plait pairs make a picot at *c*. Work a half-stitch with the other pair of the plait and a right-hand picot at *d*. Continue working the plaits until the next crossing.

Working the lace

In this pattern all four edges will be treated as trails.

Setting in to work the top trail in both directions, Figs 10b & 10c   Hang 6 pairs across the top of the pricking from left to right, as when starting Pattern 4 (Fig 4e), and anchor to one side, looping round a pin. These will be the edge trail passive pairs.

Note that along the inside edge every other pin-hole is set slightly away from the trail. These will be used for hanging in new pairs for the ground. The pin-holes closer to the trails are winkie pins.

54

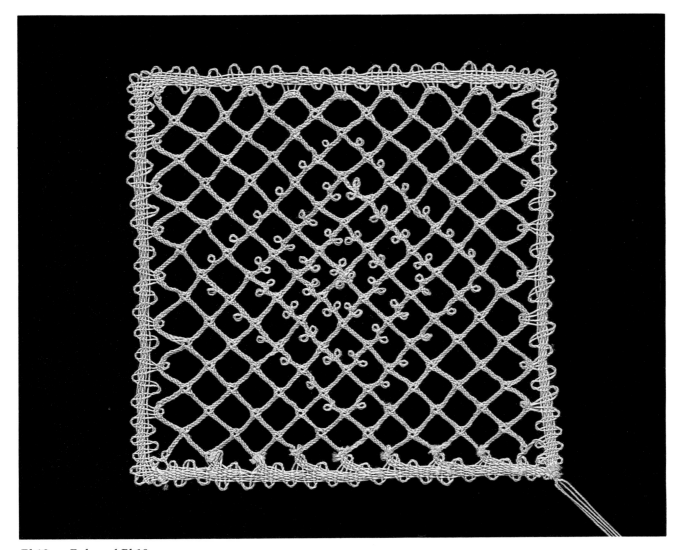

Pl 10a   *Enlarged Pl 10*

Threads are knotted and cut off before the last edge, since a large number of
pairs need to be removed.

At the last corner the workers from either side are joined and one of them
works the corner diagonally. See Fig 10e.

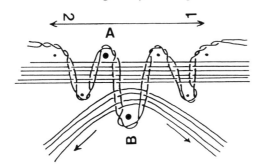

Fig 10b   *Setting in the top edge*

The pillow will need turning in opposite
directions to set in the first edge.

Choose a pin-hole on the outer edge of the trail,
A, and hang in 2 pairs. These will be the trail
worker pairs which will work the top trail to either corner, in the direction of the arrows.

Follow Fig 10c and start by turning the pillow
towards you. First work in the direction of arrow
1. Add 4 pairs at pin-hole *B* and at each of the
other offset pin-holes as shown. At pin-hole *C*
add only 2 pairs; these will work the diagonal
plait from the corner to the first row of windmill
crossings in the ground.

Turn the pillow the other way and work to pin-
hole *D*; add only 2 pairs.

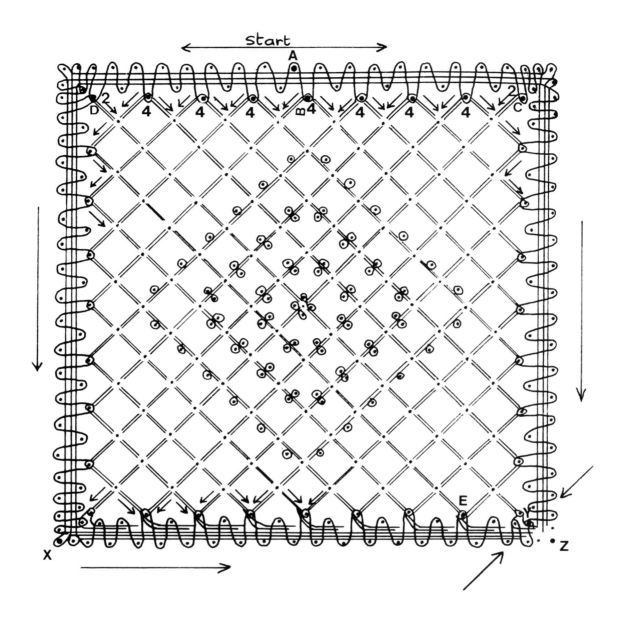

Fig 10c   *Working diagram*

Shows the direction and order of working, finishing at Z.

Note for the last edge: at each ground pin-hole just before the last edge trail, alternate threads (one from each pair) should be removed (by knotting) and the remainder taken into the trail and removed after a few rows. See also Fig 10e, pin-hole E. (prs)

Working the corners, Fig 10c On turning a corner the worker pair, as in previous patterns, becomes a passive pair for the next side, while a passive pair from the previous side becomes the new worker pair, as shown in the diagram.

Working the ground, Fig 10a & 10c Turn back the pillow, so that the pattern faces you, and work the first row of windmill crossings in the plaited ground, following the little arrows. Continue down the pattern as indicated by the two arrows, working the edge trails, making plaits, windmill crossings and picots as shown. Work the Bedfordshire blossom in the centre and continue to the last row of windmill crossings.

Working the last edge X to Z, Fig 10c-10e The two remaining corners and the edge between them need special attention. You need to keep the number of pairs in the trail even, and match its appearance to the other three, while removing a large number of pairs from it.

At corner *X* take the 2 plait pairs into the trail singly at different pin-holes; one before the corner, the other after, as shown. Lay back their threads gradually, after you turn the corner.

The other plaits join the trail 4 pairs at a time, which is cumbersome. The following approach is suggested (see Fig 10e). Knot and lay back 2 threads from each plait, very close to the pin-hole at which they are due to be taken into the trail, as at *E* for example. At the same pin-hole join the two remaining pairs into the trail and remove them after several rows, as shown.

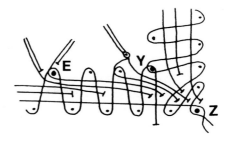

Fig 10e *Detail for the 4th corner Z, and finishing*

As for Fig 10c alternate threads should be removed from each pair and laid back, but to simplify the diagram complete pairs are shown removed.

At pin-hole *Y*, the workers from adjacent sides join. One of them continues to the last pin-hole *Z*, working diagonally across the corner pairs which are removed until only two remain. (prs)

Finishing, Figs 10c & 10e At *Y*, join the workers from either edge: twist once, work a cloth stitch, twist once more, place the pin and work another cloth stitch. With the left-hand pair work across the corner passives and lay back, as shown. With the right-hand worker work across the corner through passive pairs from either side (Fig 10e), laying back pairs so that only two remain at the last pin-hole, *Z*. Carefully trim off the laid back pairs. Knot the two remaining pairs together and use their threads to join the lace to that of Pattern 9 (Fig 10f).

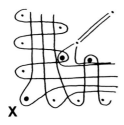

Fig 10d *Detail for the 3rd corner X*

The two pairs from the plait are taken into the corner at separate pin-holes. (prs)

Pieces with no thread specified were worked in Madeira Tanne 50 white.

Top shelf Ring of floral leaves (Pattern 15), worked in pale blue by Pat Rowley. Framed medallion, Flower No 4 (Patter 17), worked with raised rolled tallies by Anne-Marie Desrousseaux. Pendant, Flower No 1 (Pattern 17) with boxe pin-holes & Bookmark (Pattern 16), both worked in pale blue by Pat Rowley. Framed oval medallion (Pattern 13a) Madeira Tanne 30; Bookmark (Pattern 2) in Madeira Tanne 30; Framed square insertion (Pattern 10): all three worked the author.

   Lower shelf, at back Greetings card (Pattern 18) & Small greetings card (Patterns 1 & 2) in Madeira Tanne 30, bo worked by the author. Bookmark (Pattern 19), slightly modified and worked by Vi Bullard (see Additional prickings).

Lower shelf, foreground Handkerchief border (displayed right to left), worked by Janet Tarbox (Additional prickings). ...eart-shaped bonnet back, worked in Kinkame silk by Pat Rowley (Additional prickings). Earrings, Leaves *1 & 3* (Pattern ...); Pendant, Flower 2 (Pattern 17); Ring cushion (Patterns 7-10), in Madeira Tanne 50 écru: all three worked by ...nne-Marie Desrousseaux. White handkerchief with elaborate border (Pattern 12), worked by Dorothy Formston. ...owered handkerchief with coloured border (Pattern 11) in pale mauve & White handkerchief (Pattern 6), both worked ... the author. Coloured bookmark (Pattern 4), worked in shades of purple Mulberry silk by the author. Bookmark or ...sertion (Pattern 18), worked in pink by the author.

...yling Caryl Mossop and Betta Zanotto. *Display unit* Pine Antiques, 10 Market Place, Olney, Bucks. *Photo* Les Goodey.

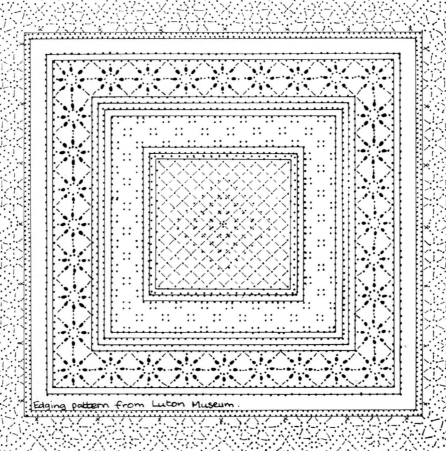

Fig 10f   *Assembly diagram for ring cushion cover, Patterns 7 to 10*

The diagram shows how Patterns 7 to 10 fit together. The outer edging is made a little larger so that it can be eased onto the next piece and form a slight frill. The pieces should be joined in slip stitch. (slightly reduced)

60

Pl 10b   *Assembled lace for ring cushion cover, Patterns 7 to 10*

Pl 11

Techniques

Working a secondary trail, Figs 11a & 11b When working a secondary trail it is important to make it slightly narrower to distinguished it from the main trail.

Leave out the pairs required to start the secondary trail at the two pin-holes c & c_1. As the worker, take the outer pair from the side opposite the first trail pin-hole, in this case c.

If there are not enough pairs in the main trail you need to add new pairs at the beginning of the secondary trail, at pin-holes c & c_1 in this case. Fig 11a shows 2 pairs added at pin-hole c and 1 pair at pin-hole c_1. Three is the minimum number of pairs with which to form a trail.

On completing the secondary trail, join it into the main trail at two separate pin-holes, f & f_1, as shown in Figs 11a & 11c. With the main trail worker pair, work in cloth stitch through the pair at f, twist once, place the pin, and work through the trail again in cloth stitch. Repeat at pin-hole f_1 for the two remaining pairs of the secondary trail.

Pattern 11
Edging with multiple trails

In this lesson the lace-maker will take an important further step towards mastering traditional Bedfordshire lace; the working of multiple trails. The pattern includes a headside trail, and a central trail with a small secondary trail enclosing it, forming a circular shape. This combination of trails is often found in Bedfordshire lace designs.

The pricking is in two versions; the original, and a slightly enlarged version from which the lace sample was made. It has been adapted, with the addition of a corner, from a pricking in the collection of Luton Museum.

Introducing Adding and leaving out pairs for a secondary trail, distinguishing a main and secondary trail by making the secondary thinner, joining a secondary trail into a main trail.

Materials 30 pairs of bobbins + 6 pairs for the corner: for the original DMC Fil à Broder machine 50, or Madeira Tanne 50; for the enlarged version DMC Fil à Broder machine 30, or Madeira Tanne 30.

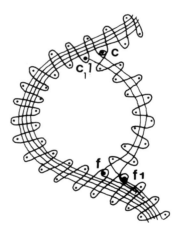

Fig 11a *Working a secondary trail*

If not enough pairs are available in the main trail to leave out for the secondary trail, hang on pairs at pin-holes c and c_1. Take the worker pair from the side opposite the first trail pin-hole.

When the trail re-joins the main trail it is taken in at two separate pin-holes. (prs)

Working the lace

Setting in and working the first head, Fig 11b Set in the footside by hanging 2 pairs on pin *A* (edge pair and worker pair). Hang 4 pairs side by side on a temporary pin above *A*; leave out 2 of these pairs for the plait after the next pin-hole. Work down 5 pin-holes of the footside and leave aside.

Set in the main trail at *B*. Hang on 7 pairs side by side on a temporary pin above it; one for the worker pair and 6 as passives: 2 of these pairs will leave immediately to work a plait for the ground.

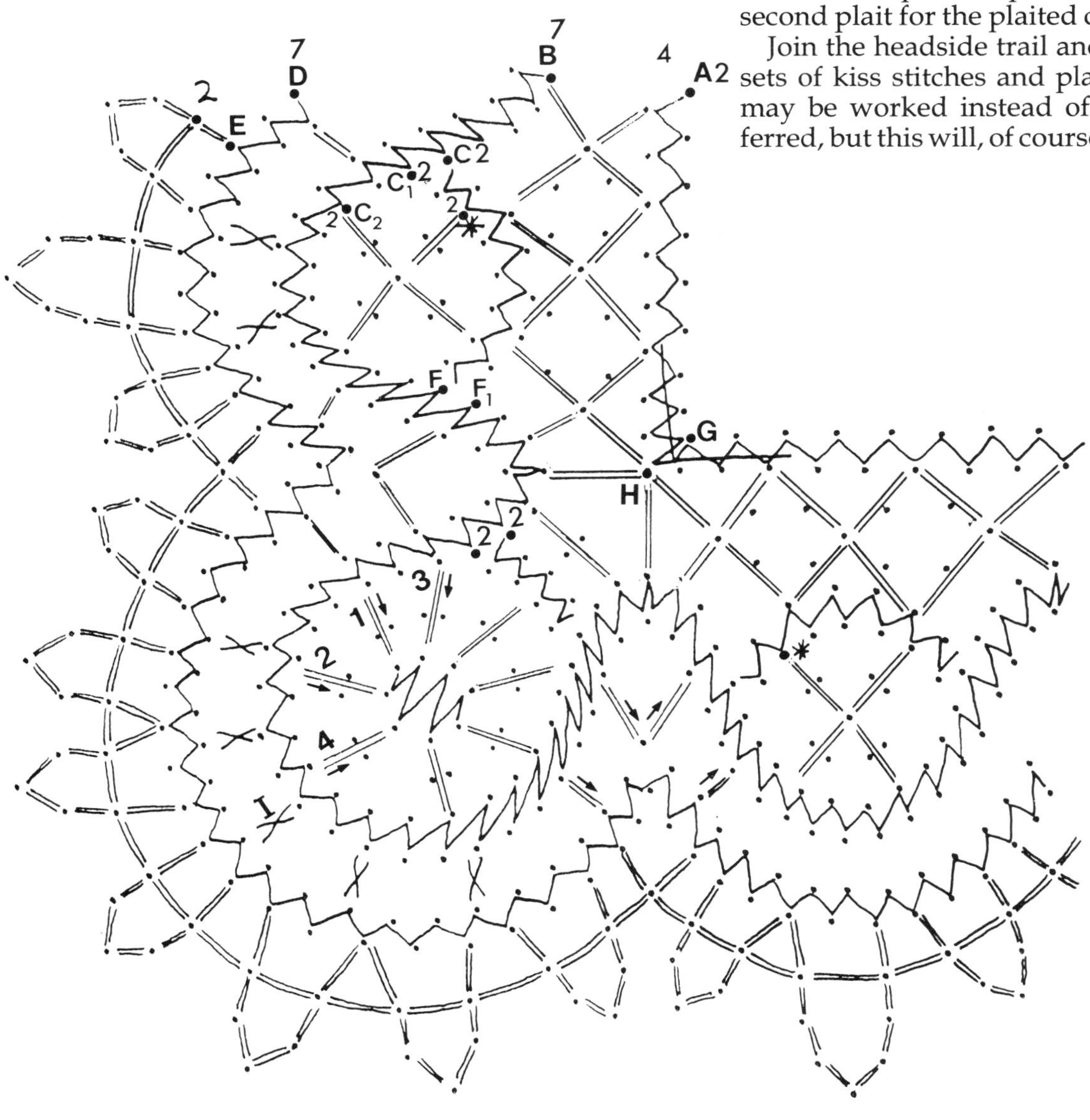

Work to pin-hole *C*, add 2 pairs, continue to pin-hole C_1 and add another 2 pairs. The 4 pairs just added will form the secondary trail (one worker and 3 passives). Add 2 more pairs at the pin-hole marked *, for the plaited centre; repeat at the corresponding pin-hole on subsequent heads, as shown.

Set in the headside trail at *D*. Hang on 7 pairs side by side on a temporary pin above it; one for the worker pair, 4 as passives, and 2 pairs which you will leave out immediately to work the plait to the main trail, to the right. At pin-hole *E* leave out 2 pairs and start the ninepin edge. At the next pin-hole add 2 pairs for the ninepin bar; hanging them on a temporary pin and working a windmill crossing.

After setting in the ninepin return to the main trail. Add 2 pairs at pin C_2; they will make the second plait for the plaited centre.

Join the headside trail and the main trail with sets of kiss stitches and plaits, as shown. Plaits may be worked instead of kiss stitches if preferred, but this will, of course, require more pairs.

Fig 11b *Working diagram* (prs)

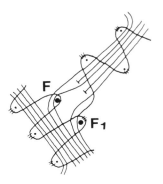

Fig 11c
Taking a secondary trail into a main trail

The pairs are taken in at two separate pin-holes. The two surplus pairs, which are removed before the join, will be replaced in each head at the * shown on Fig 11b. (prs)

Pl 11a   *Enlarged corner from Pl 11: connecting parallel trails*

Parallel trails can be joined by kiss stitches or plaits. Plaits are firmer but require more pairs than kiss stitches; often both techniques are combined, as here.

To take the secondary trail into the main trail follow Fig 11c, also Figs 11a&b. Lay back 2 pairs from the secondary trail just before joining; remember to lay back alternate threads. This leaves 4 pairs which you will join into the main trail, 2 at each pin-hole F & F_1.

Work the inside point of the headside trail as the join between the scalloped heads in Pattern 5, Figs 5b or 5c.

Working the corner, Figs 11b & 11d Work the lace until it is level with pin-holes G, H & I. Extra pairs will be needed to work the centre plaits and bud. By now you will be able to judge whether the trail contains enough pairs to leave some out for the plaits, or whether you need to add extra pairs for this. Note how many pairs you added at the top half of the trail so that you can lay back the same number from the lower part and avoid having too many.

Follow the direction of the arrows and the numbers on the diagram to work the corner plaits and the first half of the half-stitch bud.

Note the way the ninepins are worked round the headside: to cover the curve evenly some leave the trail immediately, while others remain in the trail until the next pin-hole.

Follow Fig 11d to work the inner corner, where pin-hole G will need to be used twice. At pin-hole

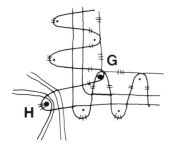

Fig 11d
Working the inner corner, pin-holes G-H (prs)

H take in the pairs from the two plaits and leave them out immediately to work the trail and plaited ground of the next side.

Continue round the pattern, lifting and moving the lace up the pricking when necessary.

Finishing To finish the border follow instructions for Pattern 1.

Pattern 12

Border with trails, leaf sprays and the Bedfordshire circle

This is a more elaborate medium-sized Bedfordshire border with a one-way design. It introduces one of the most important features of Bedfordshire lace; the Bedfordshire circle. The technique of dividing and re-joining clothwork areas to form a circle is the basis of the floral motifs in the more advanced designs.

The pricking is copied, with an additional corner, from a draft in the Luton Museum collection. The one-way design presents a new challenge when a corner is required since the normal technique of reversing it and working a mirror image cannot be applied.

As a first exercise in working one-way designs I have created a corner by adding an extended spray, to match the existing motif. You will see a different solution in Pattern 13, where it *is* possible to reverse the design.

From this pattern onwards, the number of pairs quoted should be taken as approximate. Individual lace-makers like different densities of clothwork: some prefer a solid texture, others a more open one, and this will determine the number of bobbins needed. A compromise is usually necessary to balance the effort of adding and taking out lots of pairs against achieving the desired result.

Introducing   The Bedfordshire circle, joining and dividing trails.

Materials Approx. 40 pairs of bobbins: Madeira Tanne 50, or DMC Retors d'Alsace 50

Pl 12

65

Techniques

The Bedfordshire cloth stitch circle, Fig 12a A clothwork area is divided and joined up again to form a circle, with an open centre or a filling of crossed plaits or tallies.

Begin at *a*, at the top of the outer ring of pin-holes. If no free pairs are available, hang in 2 new pairs. Work a cloth stitch, twist once, place the pin, and work another cloth stitch. Let one of the pairs drop as a passive pair and use the other as the worker pair to work from pin-hole to pin-hole, through the passives, as shown by the worker lines. Add pairs as necessary and continue to the top pin-hole at the inner circle, *x*.

Work across half of the passive pairs plus one pair, twist once, place the pin, work a cloth stitch, and twist once more. The two sides will now be worked separately. With the left-hand pair work the left side of the circle and with the right-hand pair the right side. Make sure the worker pair works at 90° to the footside.

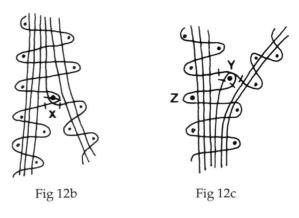

Fig 12b   Fig 12c

Fig 12b *Dividing trails*

The dividing pin-hole *x* can also be used to hang on extra pairs. (prs)

Fig 12c *Joining trails*

The first pin-hole worked after the join must be the higher one, *z*. (prs)

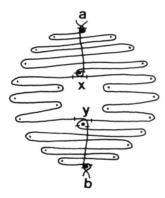

Fig 12a *Bedfordshire cloth stitch circle*

The clothwork area is divided at *x* and re-joined at *y*. (prs)

Work the two sides separately until level with pin-hole *y*, where the two workers are brought together and the clothwork is again worked as one. Twist the workers once, work a cloth stitch, twist once more, place the pin, and work another cloth stitch. Drop one of the pairs as a passive and use the other as a worker. Work from side to side. As the circle narrows leave out pairs that were added until you reach pin-hole *b*, where the two pairs will come together again.

Dividing trails, Fig 12b Where a trail divides, work to the joint pin-hole *x*, across the appropriate number of passive pairs. Twist both the worker pair and the passive pair just worked, place pin *x* between them, work a cloth stitch, and twist once. Now take each of these pairs as workers, one for the left-hand and one for the right-hand trail.

Pin-hole *x* can also be used to hang on extra pairs if there are not enough in one of the trails.

Joining trails, Fig 12c Where trails join to continue as one, the workers from each trail will meet at a pin-hole and continue as follows.

Twist each pair once, work a cloth stitch, twist once more, place the pin between them, and work another cloth stitch; leave one pair as a passive. Continue by working towards the side where the pin-hole (*z* in this case) is higher up the pattern.

Working the lace

Setting in and working the first head, Figs 12d & 12e Start at the footside. Hang in 6 pairs side by side on a temporary pin above *A*; 4 passive, 1 for the edge pair and 1 as the worker. The more prominent footside here is needed to balance the rest of the design.

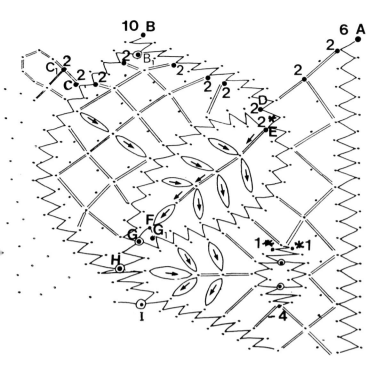

Fig 12d   *Working diagram*

In each head pairs must be added at pin-holes marked *. Those added for the circle will be removed at the bottom of the circle.

Ringed pin-holes show the position where trails join or divide. (prs)

Set in the main trail at *B*. Hang 10 pairs side by side on a temporary pin; this trail will almost immediately divide into two trails, one to the left along the headside (the headside trail), the other to the right of the leaf shape. A secondary trail will run to the left of the leaf shape, from pin-hole *D* down to pin-hole *H*.

Follow Figs 12d & 12e. With the right-hand pair as the worker, work in cloth stitch for three rows, to the ringed pin-hole B_1. Divide the main trail (Fig 12b).

Work the separate trails in cloth stitch, to pin-holes *C* & *D*, adding two extra pairs for the plaited ground at each of the pin-holes shown.

Set in the ninepin edge at pin-hole *C*. Hang in 2 pairs, and 2 further pairs at C_1. Work across the pattern, building up the headside trail, the ground and the footside, towards pin-hole *D*. Just before pin-hole *D* join the plait from the footside ground into the trail.

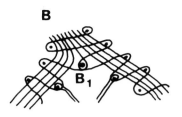

Fig 12e   *Setting in at pin-hole B* (prs)

Working the leaf shape and spray, Figs 12d & 12f
The leaf shape is outlined by two trails: the continuation of the main trail, curving slightly to the right of pin-hole *E* and then down to pin-hole *H* where it rejoins the headside trail. It continues in this way down the pattern, sweeping from left to right. The secondary trail starts from pin-hole *E*, curves to the left and down to pin-hole *H*, to form the upper and left-hand part of the leaf shape.

Add 2 pairs each at *D* & *E*, for the upper half of the leaf shape (Fig 12d), noting that pin-hole *E*, where several operations begin, needs special attention.

The * at *E* indicates that you must add 2 pairs at this pin-hole for every head. Also 2 pairs should be left out at *E* to start working the plaits of the leaf spray.

Start the secondary trail from *E*, working to the left. Take in pairs from the headside ground and leave out pairs for 3 tallies in the leaf spray, as shown by the arrows. Also from *E* make a plait for the stalk with the two pairs left out there. Work a windmill crossing with the pairs from the top tally. Continue the secondary trail and the central stalk, working windmill crossings with the two other tallies, to form the upper part of the leaf spray.

Make the three matching tallies for the lower part of the spray.

Now work the main trail to the right of pin-hole *E*, taking in the pairs from the tallies worked in the direction of the arrows, and leave out pairs for the footside ground.

Work the tip of the central stalk as a tally, to pin-hole *F*. This section also needs special attention and is shown enlarged in Fig 12f.

Pin-hole *F* has been set away from pin-hole *G* to provide enough space for the tally pairs, which must leave singly to two different pin-holes, *G* & G_1.

After placing pin *F*, work the two pairs together in cloth stitch and twist each pair enough to reach pin-holes *G* & *G₁*. Take in the pair at G_1 first and work the main leaf trail to pin-hole *G*. Work the secondary trail to pin-hole *G* and take into the trail the second pair from *F*. Also at *G* join the two trails by working the join between the two worker pairs, i.e. twist each pair once, work a cloth stitch, twist once more, place the pin, and work another cloth stitch.

Continue as one trail up to pin-hole *H*. At *H* work another join, as at *G*, with the worker pair from the headside trail and the worker pair from the main leaf trail. Follow Fig 12f. Keep pulling down the passives to avoid a seersucker effect,

and leave out pairs for the tally in the horizontal spray on the right, and for the ninepin on the left.

Work as one trail to pin-hole *I*. Divide here into two trails to start the next head, as you did at the beginning at pin-hole B_1.

Working the circle, Fig 12d & 12g Follow the enlarged diagram to see how the pairs work through the circle. Add single pairs at the two pin-holes * and repeat for each circle in the pattern. Hang the pair on a temporary pin; work a cloth stitch with the worker pair, place pin *, twist three times, and work another cloth stitch. Work to the left through the passives and repeat for the second pin-hole *. Work through the circle following the diagram, separating the clothwork at pin-hole *x* and rejoining it at *y*. Take in and leave out pairs as shown. At the bottom of the circle remove 4 pairs and repeat the operation at this position for every circle in the pattern. Remember to lay back alternate threads.

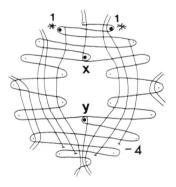

Fig 12g
Enlarged Bedfordshire circle

At pin-holes marked * add 1 extra pair in each head. Remove 4 pairs at the bottom. Pin-holes *x* & *y* show where the clothwork divides and re-joins. (prs)

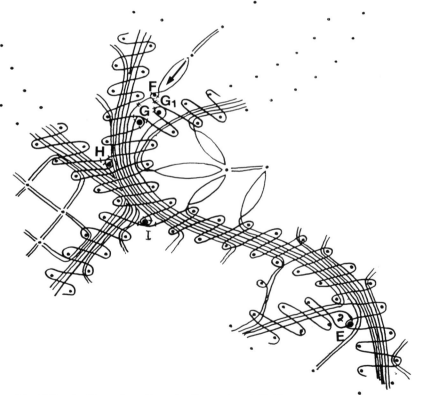

Fig 12f   *Section where three trails meet and divide*

There are 15 pairs at the widest part of the trail just below pin-hole *H*, and not all can be shown. It is not worth removing pairs as they will be needed almost immediately for the next head. Pull the passives down frequently and firmly to maintain the tension and texture. (prs)

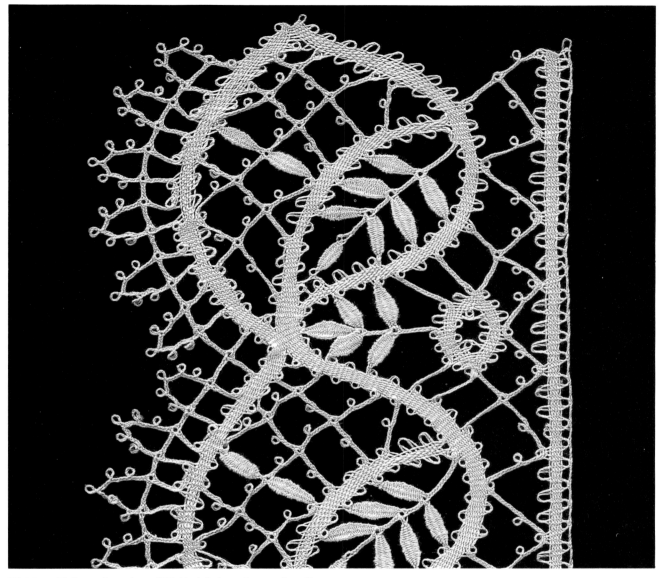

Pl 12a *Enlarged section of Pl 12: joining of several trails*

Special care is needed to work this section as there are 15 pairs at the widest
part of the join.

Working the corner, Figs 12h & 12i As you can
see from the direction of the arrows in Fig 12h
you will need to turn the pillow several times;
make sure the work is always facing you.

Work to the inner corner at pin-hole K. Work in
cloth stitch through 4 pairs of passives, twist
three times, and place pin K_1; work back across
the four passives and leave the worker pair as a
passive for the next side.

Take the first passive pair worked through as
the worker pair, and take in the plait pairs from
the right-hand side of the circle. Work in cloth
stitch across the plait pairs; twist the workers 3
times, place pin L, work in cloth stitch across 5
pairs (2 plait and 3 footside passives) and leave as
a passive for the next side.

The plait pairs taken in at L will be left out immediately (see arrow in Figs 12h & 12i) to work a plait, then a windmill crossing with the incoming pairs from the lower part of the circle, then another plait before they are joined into the main trail. *Note* Pin-hole L (Fig 12i) is used twice for two separate operations.

Leave the inner corner and work the headside and ground as far as the diagonal corner line. Work the leaf-shape trail to M, as in previous heads, following the arrows. Note that you will need to leave out pairs, or add extra pairs, for the tallies of the large leaf spray, which will be worked from pin-hole M to L. Some lace-makers will prefer to remove surplus pairs from the trail, adding extra pairs for the tallies towards the end

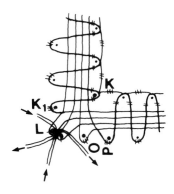

Fig 12i *Working the inner corner*

Pin-hole L is worked twice. After completing the corner pull the threads firmly. Pin-holes O and P are worked after the pillow has been turned. (prs)

Fig 12h *Corner leaf trails and spray*

Follow the arrows and letters for the order of working. Turn the pillow so that you work facing the lace straight on. (prs)

of the spray when no pairs from the trail are available. Other lace-makers may prefer to add pairs for the tallies at the beginning of the spray, to keep the line of the trail intact as long as possible.

When joining the leaf-shape trail remove pairs so that only two pairs remain at pin-hole M. With these two pairs and the plait pairs from the ground work a windmill crossing at pin-hole M: this then becomes the tip of the leaf spray. Work the tally to N with the two pairs, and with the two others work a plait to the main trail.

With the pairs left out from the leaf-shape trail and those added, work the ten tallies on one side of the stalk. Using the pairs from N, work plaits and 9 windmill crossings with the pairs from the tallies to form the stalk itself. At the tenth tally work a six-pair crossing (see Pattern 2).

Work the last stalk plait to pin L. With the second footside passive from the left as a worker pair, work in cloth stitch to take in the plait pairs, using pin-hole L again. The plait pairs just taken in leave immediately to work a plait for the ground.

With the worker pair from L work in cloth stitch through the two remaining passive pairs and leave as a passive pair for the next side. Twist the first of the two passive pairs worked through 3 times: it becomes a worker pair for one stitch. Place pin O, work a cloth stitch with the pair to the right and leave it as a passive for the next side. Twist the passive pair just worked through 3 times, place pin P and use this pair as the worker pair for the next side.

Work the ten tallies for the other half of the leaf spray, starting with the one near the tip of the stalk and working towards the inner corner as shown by the arrow. Complete the corner headside and take the tally pairs into the main trail to start the first head of the next side.

Finishing To finish the border follow instructions for Pattern 1.

Pl 13

Pattern 13

Circular border and oval motif with leaf shapes

This pattern introduces the working of solid areas of cloth stitch, here formed into leaves with simple veins where you can practice adding pairs in three different ways.

With this pattern you will have reached a level of skill which will allow you to decide whether to create a close-textured clothwork or a more open one. This will determine the number of pairs needed: the number given below is only approximate.

The pricking has been adapted from a parchment in the collection of Bedford Museum. One head has been arranged into a small motif as an alternative.

Introducing Leaf shapes of solid clothwork with veins in different positions, adding and removing pairs to form different clothwork shapes.

Materials 34 or more pairs of bobbins: for the circular border Madeira Tanne 30, or DMC Retors d'Alsace 30, or Linen 120; for the oval motif Gutermans silk.

Techniques

Leaves and veins Leaves are a common feature in Bedfordshire lace and are represented in various forms, from simple sprays of tallies outlined by trails (shown in previous patterns), to solid areas of clothwork with veins resembling specific leaves, some of which are included in this and the following patterns.

Leaves appear in different positions in relation to the footside and will be worked differently in each. The position of the leaf in the pattern will also determine the position of the vein (or veins) and this needs special attention.

All leaves must be started at the highest point on the pattern and must be worked at an angle of 90° to the footside, with passives running as nearly as possible parallel to the footside.

In this pattern you will practice working a simple leaf shape with a single vein in both vertical and horizontal positions; the near-vertical will be treated as vertical.

The upright leaf This is the simpler one to work. Adding a vertical vein will not make it more difficult.

The leaf is worked in cloth stitch and extra pairs are added at the sides as the shape widens, to maintain a firm texture. The technique for adding pairs at the edge of a clothwork shape is described below. At the base of the leaf pairs must be laid back so that just enough remain to continue the pattern.

The horizontal leaf The flattened curve at the top will require extra pairs which cannot be added at the side of the clothwork like the upright leaf. The technique for adding pairs is given below.

Veins Veins are worked in different ways according to their angle to the footside and the amount of definition required. Leaves come with either single or multiple veins and this too affects the method of working.

In this pattern the leaves have single veins, either vertical or horizontal. The vertical veins are obtained by twisting the worker pair; the horizontal ones by twisting the passive pairs. The near-vertical veins are worked like the vertical ones.

Adding pairs to areas of clothwork When working solid areas of clothwork as in this and the following patterns, you will have to add pairs to suit the shape, and to create the desired texture and keep it even. Pairs are usually added singly at the edge of a shape as it widens, but sometimes this is not enough and other techniques have to be used, as explained below.

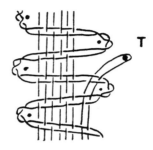

Fig 13a
*Adding one pair to a
clothwork edge*

Fig 13b
*Adding pairs in twos for a
line of clothwork*

Fig 13c
*Combining methods from
Figs 13a & 13b*

72

Adding pairs singly at the side of a clothwork area, Fig 13a   Hang the extra pair on a temporary pin above the edge pin-hole. Work in cloth stitch with the worker pair, place the pin, twist the worker three times, work again in cloth stitch and continue the row through the passives. Remove the temporary pin and ease the threads down into the clothwork, as in Pattern 6, Fig 6e, pin-hole *E*.

This is used in Leaf *1*.

Adding pairs in twos to create a width of clothwork, Fig 13b   Place a row of pins and hang two pairs, straddled, on each; twist each pair as many times as the twists on the winkie pins in the other parts of the pattern. Work through the added pairs as across passives. This technique is used to start Leaf *3*. Although pairs from incoming plaits are used the same principle applies.

Combining the two methods of adding pairs, Fig 13c Sometimes pairs will have to be added, in twos, for the shallow curve at the top (Fig 13b) *as well as singly* at the side of a clothwork shape, from a temporary pin (Fig 13a). In such cases combine both techniques: this will avoid unsightly gaps in the fabric as indicated by * in Leaf *3*.

Pattern 13a
Circular border

Working the lace

This is another circular pattern and the clothwork passives should be kept as near parallel to the footside edge as possible. Remember that the pillow must be turned regularly to maintain the correct angle. It may be helpful to imagine that the centre of the circle is an extension of the footside and to use this radius line as a guide for the working rows. It is also useful to place the cover cloth on this line and move it frequently.

Setting in and working the first head, Fig 13d Start with the headside trail. Hang 4 pairs side by side on a temporary pin above *A*: 3 for the passives and one as the worker pair. As you work down the headside add 2 pairs at each of the 5 trail pin-holes shown, for plaits.

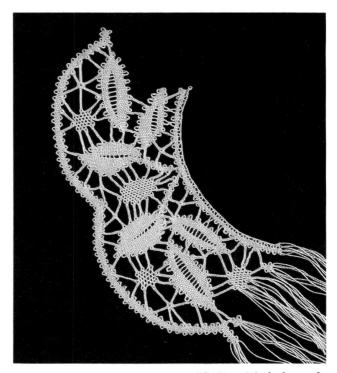

Pl 13a   *Worked sample*

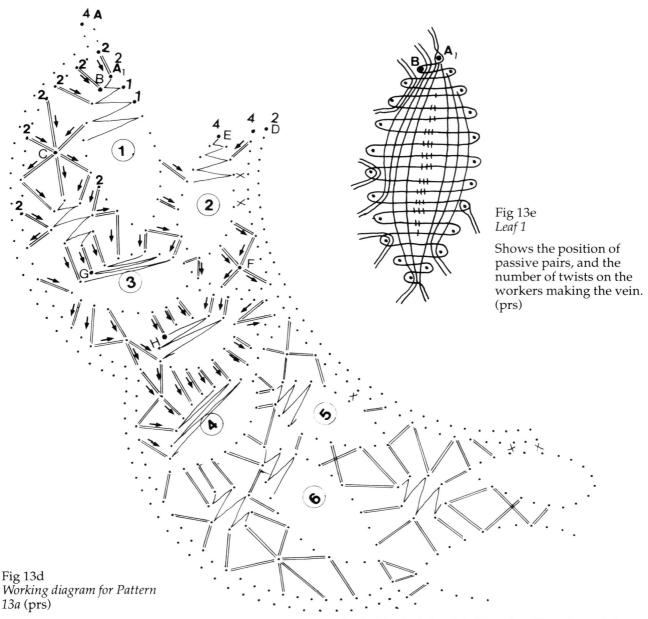

Fig 13e
Leaf 1

Shows the position of passive pairs, and the number of twists on the workers making the vein. (prs)

Fig 13d
Working diagram for Pattern 13a (prs)

Leaf 1 With the first two added pairs work a plait to A_1, to begin leaf 1. Hang two more pairs on a temporary pin above A_1. With the right-hand pair from the plait work in cloth stitch through these pairs, twist twice and place pin A_1. Work to the left through three pairs and through the two pairs from the next plait; place pin B. Work to the right, adding the first of the 2 *single* pairs at the right-hand edge of the leaf as shown. Work down the leaf, and the headside, working plaits, taking their pairs into the leaf, and leaving out others as indicated by the arrows.

With the plait pairs from the headside and the leaf work a six-pair crossing at pin-hole C. Work the half-stitch bud; follow the direction of the arrows to take in and leave out pairs.

Start the vertical vein down the middle of the leaf at about the fifth working row (Fig 13e). At the centre of the row twist the workers once; repeat at the same position in the next row. Increase the twists to two and then to three on subsequent rows as the leaf widens. Decrease the number of twists towards the bottom of the leaf, and as the leaf narrows lay back pairs to the back of the pillow so that only 4 pairs finally remain to work the two plaits to leaves 2 & 3.

For the footside hang 4 pairs side by side on a temporary pin above D and 2 pairs, straddled, on D: 4 passive pairs, 1 edge pair and 1 worker pair.

Work several rows and leave out two pairs for a plait to Leaf 2.

Leaf 2 This leaf is also worked as a vertical one. Hang in 4 pairs, straddled, over pin *E*. Twist the right-hand pair and work in cloth stitch first to the left and then to the right, and so on. Join to the footside with two kiss stitches.

Make the central vein in the same way as for leaf 1. Follow the arrows: take in plait pairs from the lower part of leaf *1* and leave out others to join the footside, leaf No 3 and the four-plait crossing at pin-hole *F*. At the lower part of the leaf lay back pairs so that again only 4 pairs remain at the end.

Leaf 3, Figs 13d & 13f This is a horizontal leaf and will have to be started with a long row of cloth stitch.

Place pins between the incoming plait pairs (Fig 13f). Take the left-hand of the plait pairs at *G* as the worker pair and work to the right in cloth stitch through the pairs of the next 4 plaits. Continue working the rows as shown, taking in the other incoming plait pairs at the sides. The two positions marked * may need an extra pair, added as shown in Fig 13c. At the half-way row form the

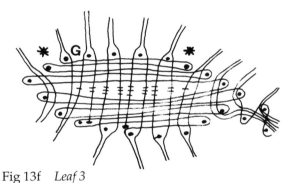

Fig 13f *Leaf 3*

Start the leaf at *G*. An extra pair may be needed at pin-holes marked *. Follow Fig 13c. (prs)

central vein, starting from the left: twist the passives, first once, then twice and, in the middle of the row, three times; decrease the number of twists towards the right, as shown in the diagram. This will produce the same effect as the veins in the vertical leaves.

Do not be tempted to cram too many rows of cloth stitch into the lower part of this leaf, or the vein may loose its definition. Leave out pairs for the plaits to connect to the other parts of the pattern, and for the stalk trail.

Finish the leaf as you began, placing the pins between the pairs on the shallow curve; make sure that they are placed at the right pin-holes for the next set of plaits (see Fig 13f). Lay back unwanted pairs, taking alternate threads.

Work the stalk trail, the headside trail and the footside, and remember to gradually turn the pillow as you work so that the passive pairs are at about 90° to the footside.

Next work the oval half-stitch bud. Start at pin-hole *H*, on a straight line across the pairs of the four incoming plaits: 3 from the leaf and 1 from the stalk. Work in half-stitch following the row markings, taking in plait pairs and leaving out pairs for the next head.

Leaves *4, 5 & 6* of the next head are a mirror image of those in the first head, but are worked in the same way.

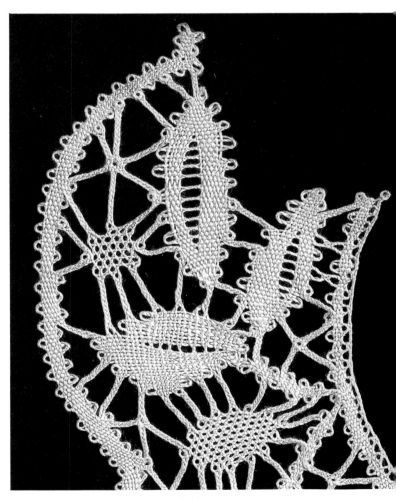

Pl 13b *Enlarged section of P13*

Note Leaf 3 which begins with a long row of cloth stitch worked with incoming plait pairs.

Pattern 13b

Oval motif

Working the lace

To set in the the curved edge follow instructions
and Figs 4e-g in Pattern 4. Work the three leaves
as in Pattern 13 and note the slight modification
of the pricking.

To finish the curved trail at the bottom of the
motif, follow instructions and Figs 14g & 14h for
the medallions in the next pattern.

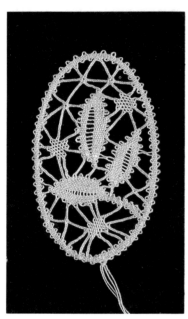

Pl 13c

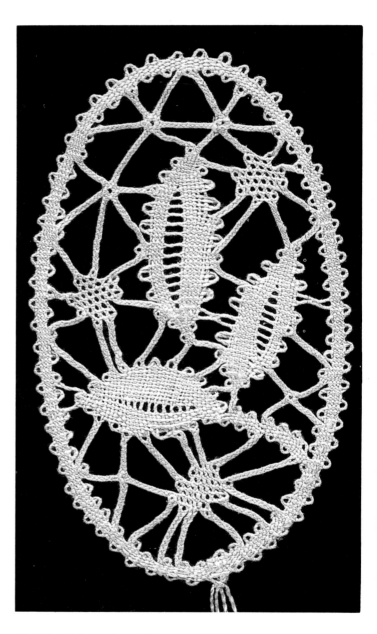

Pl 13d   *Enlarged medallion from Pl 13c*

Note how the pattern was adapted to the oval
medallion, with an extra half-stitch bud and ground
leading into the first leaf.

76

Pattern 14

Five single leaf medallions with gimped veins and raised tallies

This is the most common of the leaf motifs found in traditional Bedfordshire patterns. The method of working a leaf varies with its position in the lace. Veins, gimps and raised tallies, often seen on these leaves, give added definition and texture. Working them will provide further practice in the techniques of Bedfordshire floral patterns.

Samples *1* to *3* show the leaf with a central vein in three different positions. The vein is worked with two rows of pin-holes. Samples *4* and *5* show leaves with a central vein outlined by a gimp, the vein being formed with one pin-hole. This is an older method of working veins which can only be worked in the two positions shown. All five samples have raised tallies.

The finished pieces of lace can be framed in medallions or brooches, made into items of jewellery such as earrings, or used as dress decorations.

Introducing The single leaf medallion; the leaf worked in three positions with veins on a double row of pin-holes, the raised tally, the gimp used for a main vein.

Materials Approx. 36 pairs of bobbins; 1 pair for the gimp in Leaves *4* and *5*: Madeira Tanne 50; Coton à Broder No 18 for the gimp.

Techniques

The raised tally, Figs 14a & 14b A raised tally is made within an area of clothwork or half-stitch and stands out from it, varying the texture. A pin-hole surrounded by a circle or a square indicates where a raised tally is to be made.

Work the clothwork area until almost level with the pin-hole and leave the workers to one side. Carefully pull all passives straight down. If the raised tally is marked in the centre of the clothwork area, count the threads and use the two centre pairs, placing a pin between them. Twist the pairs once and make a square-ended tally, its length 1½ times its width. Place a pin crosswise under the tally to lift it up a little (see Fig 14a); lodge the pin behind pins already in the

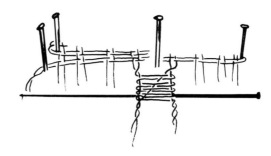

Fig 14a *First stage of a raised tally*

Start by working a square ended tally. Lift the tally a little on a pin placed crosswise.

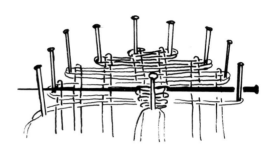

Fig 14b *Second stage of a raised tally*

Lift the tally on its holding pin and lodge it a little way back. Remove the tally pin and replace it in front.

work to prop up the tally, as shown in Fig 14b. Take out the pin from the tally pin-hole at the back and replace it in the same pin-hole from the front, and continue working. You can remove the support pin after several rows.

When the tally is off centre, pull the passives carefully down into position and use the two threads on either side of the tally pin-hole to work it.

The gimp, Figs 14c & 14d A gimp is a thicker thread worked into the edge of a motif or round some of its features to add definition. In Bedfordshire lace a gimp can be laid either outside the edge pins, as in Point Ground (Buckinghamshire lace), or inside the edge pins as in Honiton lace.

The gimp thread is wound onto a pair of bobbins and laid between the threads of a worker pair. The worker pair is twisted before and after the gimp has been laid and the edge pin placed to hold it in position.

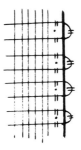

Fig 14c *Gimp outside the edge pins* (prs)

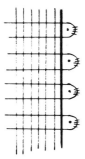

Fig 14d *Gimp inside the edge pins* (prs)

Method 1 Outside the edge pins, Fig 14c This method is used mostly for leaf and flower shapes.

Just before the edge pin-hole twist the worker twice; place the pin, lay the gimp between the threads of the worker pair (over the right and under the left) and twist the worker pair twice: place the gimp between the threads of the worker pair once more (under the left and over the right), twist the worker pair twice and continue working the row.

Method 2 Inside the edge pins, Fig 14d On a longer straight edge, a better effect is obtained by laying the gimp thread inside the edge pins, setting it tightly between the clothwork and the edge pin. It looks like the gimp in Honiton lace but unlike Honiton is made with a single thread.

Lay the gimp between the threads of the worker pair (over the right and under the left), place the pin, twist the workers three or four times (depending on thread thickness) very tightly round the pin to keep the gimp close to the clothwork, place the gimp again between the worker threads (under the left and over the right) and continue the row.

78

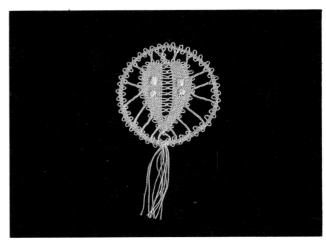

Pl 14, *Leaf 1*

Working the leaf medallions

Leaf 1, with a vertical vein of kiss stitches and raised tallies, Figs 14e-14h The stalk trail is worked up to the start of the vein; the leaf itself is then worked in two halves, joined by kiss stitches, to the end of the vein. The last part of clothwork is worked in one.

Set in the circular edge trail as for the bookmark in Pattern 4: hang in 6 pairs for the passives and 2 worker pairs at A. Work the trail in both directions. Add 2 pairs at each of the trail pin-holes shown for the plaits.

Join the two sets of pairs at B and work the short trail to form the leaf stalk. Divide the trail as

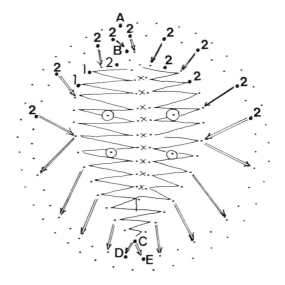

Fig 14e *Leaf 1 working diagram*

Ringed pin-holes indicate the positions of raised tallies. (prs)

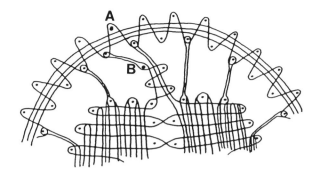

Fig 14f   *Working the top of Leaf 1*

Set in at *A* and start the stalk trail at *B*. (prs)

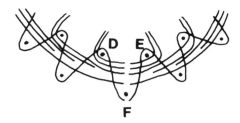

Fig 14g   *Completing the circular trail*

Lay back pairs as shown. Take the last two plaits into the edge trail at *D* and *E*. Finish at *F*. (prs)

shown and join each set of pairs into the separate halves of the leaf. One pair becomes a worker pair, the other a passive pair for the respective side.

Set in the two halves of the leaf with the pairs from the incoming plaits and the stalk. Add pairs using the technique for adding pairs on a horizontal line (Figs 13b & 13c).

Start the leaf; work the two halves separately, in cloth stitch. To link the two halves and form the vein, bring the worker pairs to the middle and work a kiss stitch between the central pin-holes, as shown. The worker pairs will have changed places.

Continue working the pattern, adding the plait pairs as the shape widens. Work the raised tallies at the ringed pin-holes. Take in and leave out plait pairs as shown. As the leaf narrows lay back passive pairs, making sure that you remove threads from just inside the edge, not an outer one.

At the lower end of the vein, join the two worker pairs as you would join trails (see Pattern 12, Fig 12c). One of the pairs becomes a passive.

Continue laying back pairs so that only four are left at pin-hole *C*. With these pairs work two plaits and take them into the trail at pin-holes *D* & *E*.

Finishing, Figs 14g & 14h   Follow the two working diagrams to complete the circular trail; the diagrams apply to all medallions. Lay back some of the trail passives so that only 4 or 5 *threads* are left on either side of the last pin-hole, *F*. Follow Fig 14h and knot these threads as they meet; place the pin, then knot together the worker pairs after twisting them several times, as shown.

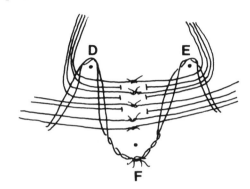

Fig 14h   *Finishing the medallion*

Tie the remaining passives together, and the workers at the last pin *F*.

Pl 14a   *Leaf 1*

The central vein is formed by kiss stitches.

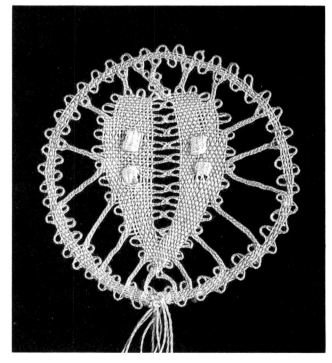

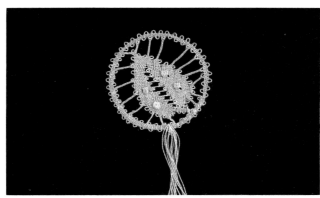

Pl 14, *Leaf 2*

Leaf 2, with a diagonal vein and raised tallies, Figs 14i & 14j   The leaf will be worked in one up to the first vein pin-hole and then in two halves, the right-hand half first. At each vein pin-hole one pair will be left out to be taken into the left half at the matching pin-hole.

Set in the circular edge trail in the same way as for Leaf 1. Work the trail and plaits and set in the top of the leaf, adding pairs on the first working row, as shown in Fig 14i.

Work the clothwork to the passive pair immediately above the first vein pin-hole, B. Twist each pair once, place pin B, work a cloth stitch, and twist once more. Leave the left-hand pair to one side to become the worker pair for the left-hand side. Continue by working the right-hand half of the leaf. At each subsequent vein pin-hole leave out the last passive pair worked, *twisted twice*. Work the raised tallies, as marked by the ringed pin-holes, after pulling down the passives evenly into position.

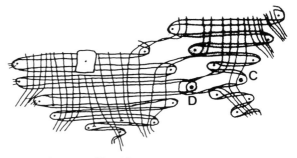

Fig 14j   *Bottom of Leaf 2*

To work the stalk leave out two pairs from the right half at *C*, and two from the left half at *D*, before completing the lower part of the leaf.

Take in and leave out pairs as shown by the arrows, so that two pairs remain at pin-hole *C* to help work the stalk trail (Fig 14i-j).

To work the vein (Fig 14i) return to pin-hole *B*. With the pair left there as the worker, work the left part of the leaf. At each vein pin-hole take in the pair left there from the right-hand half. Leave out pairs for the plaits and work the raised tallies at the ringed pin-holes. At the last vein pin-hole, *D* (Fig 14j), leave out two pairs for the stalk trail and complete the leaf, laying back pairs as the shape narrows and the pairs begin to crowd the space.

Work the stalk as a trail with 2 or 3 pairs of passives and a worker pair. Take its pairs into the circular edge trail at two adjacent pin-holes.

Complete the lace as for Leaf 1 (Figs 14g & 14h).

Pl 14b   *Leaf 2*

Each half is worked separately. The diagonal vein is worked with pairs left out from each row of the first half.

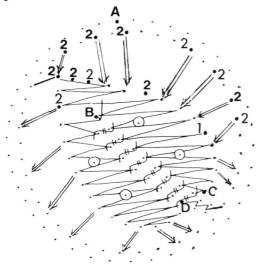

Fig 14i   *Leaf 2 working diagram* (prs)

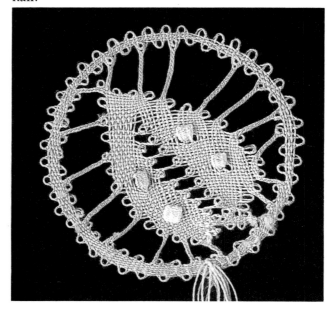

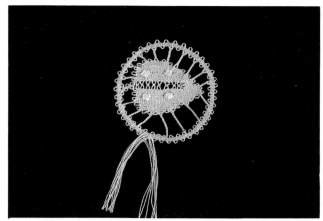

Pl 14, *Leaf 3*

Leaf 3, with a horizontal vein of upright kiss stitches and raised tallies, Figs 14k & 14l The leaf starts and ends on a shallow curve and the horizontal vein is obtained from a row of cloth stitches worked with passives, resembling kiss stitches. All will need special attention, but will add to the techniques available to you.

Begin by setting in the circular edge trail, as for the previous two leaves, following Fig 14k. Make the plaits which will lead into the top half of the leaf. Set in the leaf, bearing in mind that it begins on quite a long row of 5 pin-holes. Extra single pairs may need to be added as the leaf edge curves to the right; if so follow Fig 13c.

Work down to the first row of vein pin-holes, taking in the plait pairs and adding others as indicated. Remember to position the passives so that you obtain an even spread of threads before making the raised tallies at the ringed pin-holes.

Leave out 2 pairs at pin-hole *B* for the stalk trail.

To work the vein with upright kiss stitches (Figs 14k & 14l) place the pins at the first row of vein pin-holes so that there are 2 passive pairs between each pin. Leave some untwisted passives to the left of the first vein pin-hole, for the stalk. Twist each pair three times; work a cloth stitch with the pairs on either side of a pin, as shown; twist three times, place the second row of pins between the pairs that worked the cloth stitch. This will give the effect of a kiss stitch.

Work to pin-hole *C*, continue the row to the right, then back to the left under the entire row of vein stitches, to pin-hole *D*; leave out 2 more pairs for the stalk trail.

Continue the lower part of the leaf following Fig 14k carefully. Make the raised tallies so that they match those on the upper half.

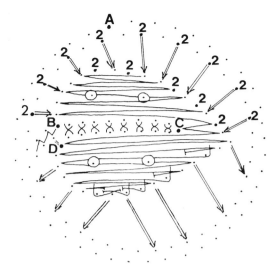

Fig 14k *Leaf 3 working diagram*

Note the working of the right-hand end of the vein, to pin-hole *C* and back under the entire row, to *D*. (prs)

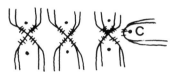

Fig 14l *Horizontal vein in upright kiss stitches*

Showing detail for pin-hole *C*.

Pl 14c *Leaf 3*

The horizontal vein is worked with upright kiss stitches.

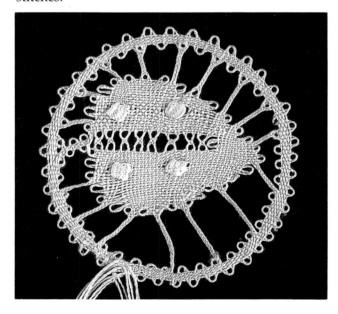

The lower part of the leaf ends on a shallow curve and is asymmetrical. Make sure that the passives are in a vertical position. If they appear to crowd together remove pairs, but remember not to remove adjacent threads nor threads on the very edge.

In the bottom part, crowding can occur towards the shallow curve and the worker pair cannot always maintain a proper outline of the shape. In that case the worker pair itself can be laid back, provided it has worked two stitches after the edge pin, and the passive pair next to it can be 'bent' into position and used as the worker. Two possible arrangements are shown in the diagrams but there may be others as no two pieces will be worked in the same way.

Complete the lace as in previous leaves.

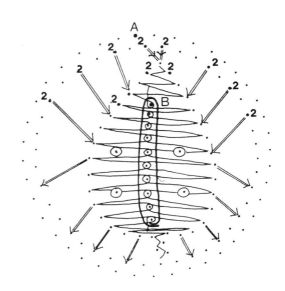

Fig 14m   *Leaf 4 working diagram* (prs)

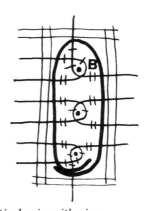

Fig 14n   *Vertical vein with gimp*

The thick line shows the position of the gimp inside the edge pin-holes. (prs)

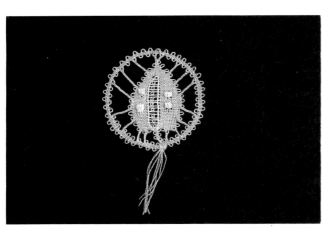

Pl 14, *Leaf 4*

Leaf 4, with a vertical vein outlined with a gimp and raised tallies, Figs 14m & 14n   Set in the circular edge trail at *A*, as for previous leaves. Make the plaits and add pairs.

Set in the leaf. Work to the end of the row *above* the vein. Next work half a row, to just before pin-hole *B*; do not work the passive above pin-hole *B* itself as it will become the worker pair for the right-hand side of the leaf.

To secure the gimp *inside* the vein pins and work the rest of the leaf (Figs 14m & 14n) follow Method 2 above (Fig 14d), but not the variation in twists. Start from the left of pin-hole *B*. Slip the gimp thread between the two threads of the worker pair and the two threads of the passive pair at pin-hole *B* (not yet worked). Twist both pairs once, work a cloth stitch with them, twist once, place pin *B*; work another cloth stitch, and twist both pairs twice. The two twists widen the vein a little. Lay the gimp between the threads of the worker pairs again and continue working.

82

Although you will use two separate workers for the clothwork on either side of the vein, the two halves will be worked simultaneously, as in Leaf 1. Join the two workers at the vein pin-hole. They could be linked by a kiss stitch, as in Leaf 1, but it is more customary to join them in the same way as at pin-hole B, except that they are twisted *twice* before the first cloth stitch, as shown in Fig 14n. Work each vein pin-hole in this way, securing the gimp on either side. You could also twist the workers between the gimp and the clothwork, as was sometimes done to save a pair of passives, but nowadays most lace-makers prefer the gimp close to the clothwork, as in Honiton lace.

Work down the leaf edge trail and plaits; make the raised tallies at the ringed pin-holes.

At the bottom of the vein, after completing the last pin-hole, cross over the gimp threads through both worker pairs and lay them back. Cut off the bobbins after working a few rows, leaving an inch or two of gimp thread to be cut off close to the fabric when the lace is completed.

After completing the last pin-hole, drop one of the worker pairs to become a passive; with the other continue and complete the leaf. Lay back pairs so that only 4 pairs remain to work the short stalk trail.

Finish the circular edge as in Leaf 1.

Pl 14, *Leaf 5*

Leaf 5, with horizontal vein outlined by a gimp, Figs 14o-14q Set in the circular edge trail and leaf as for Leaf 3. Work the upper half of the leaf, including the raised tallies, down to the vein line, as in Leaf 3.

To work the vein and gimp pull the passives well down into position and allocate one passive pair for each vein pin-hole. Work to pin-hole B and leave out 2 pairs for the stalk trail. Work back across two more pairs and leave the worker aside while you secure the gimp (following Method 2 above).

Pl 14d   *Leaf 4*

The vertical vein is outlined by a gimp.

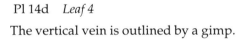

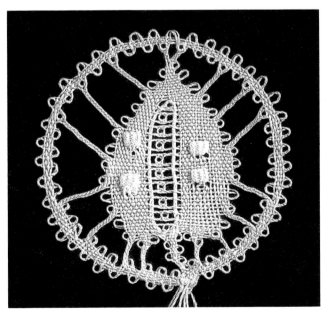

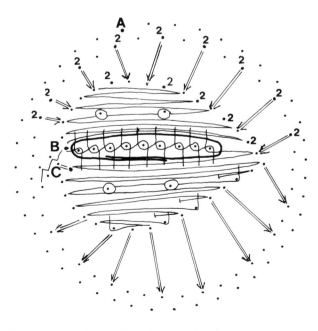

Fig 14o   *Leaf 5 working diagram* (prs)

83

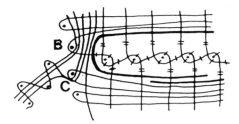

Fig 14p *Horizontal vein with gimp*

The stalk is formed with pairs from both the upper (*B*) and lower (*C*) parts of the leaf. (prs)

Lay the gimp through the threads of each of the passive pairs, and twist each pair twice (Figs 14o & 14p). Place the left end of the gimp through the threads of the worker pair and twist the pair once.

To work the vein follow Fig 14p. With the worker pair and the first passive pair work a cloth stitch, twist both pairs once, place the pin, work another cloth stitch. The worker pair becomes a passive for the lower half of the leaf and the passive pair becomes the worker pair for the next vein pin-hole. Twist the new passive pair twice and the new worker pair once, as shown. Repeat for each vein pin-hole.

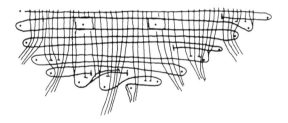

Fig 14q *Bottom of Leaf 5*

A large number of pairs must be removed. One method is shown here.

At the right-hand end of the vein, place the gimp through the threads of the worker pair. Continue to the left, laying the gimp through the threads of the vein passives just worked, up to the second pair beyond the half-way line. Do the same for the left-hand end, then lay back the gimp threads (Fig 14p).

With the worker pair continue to the right, to the end of the row, then back under the gimp thread to pin-hole *C*. At *C* leave out two pairs for the stalk trail (Fig 14p).

Finish the medallion as for Leaf 3.

Pl 14e *Leaf 5*

The gimped horizontal vein.

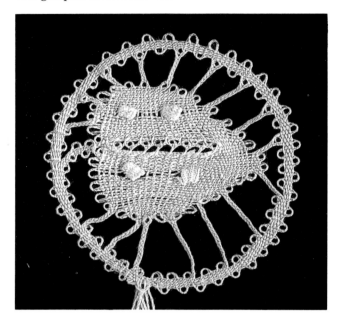

84

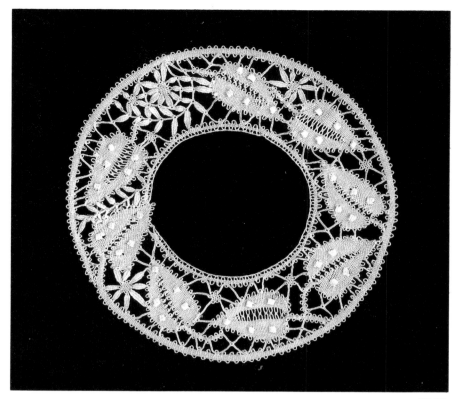

Pl 15

Pattern 15

A ring of floral leaves and tallies

This pattern is a modern interpretation of the simpler forms of floral Bedfordshire leaves. It will be followed by exercises in working side veins, and finally the flower. Many of the techniques learnt so far can now be practised together by working this ring, with a few additional tips in support. The finished lace can be mounted as a frame, a small mat, or a greetings card.

When faced with a new pattern, it will help to first colour in the solid clothwork areas with a crayon. The overall design then becomes clear and the details emerge. The ringed pin-holes mark raised tallies, the small black shapes indicate pointed tallies; the lines are plaits. The half-stitch buds are outlined by a circle of pin-holes, and some of the leaf stalks merge into the edge trail. The leaves are set in two positions, vertical and diagonal and the veins are formed by two rows of pin-holes.

Follow the arrows for the starting (also the finishing) point, and for the direction of working.

Fig 15a *Outline of the design*

An enlarged copy of the whole pricking may also be helpful.

85

Pl 15a
Enlarged section of Pl 15

Shows the leaf spray and
flower of tallies in detail.

Fig 15b
Enlarged section of pricking

Corresponds to the
enlarged photograph.

Materials Between 35 and 40 pairs of bobbins: Madeira Tanne 50.

Working the lace

Keep turning the pillow so that the working rows
are as near 90° to the footside as possible. The
footside here is related to the centre of the circle,
marked by the dot. As you turn the pillow set the
edge of the cover cloth on the radius line, across
to the centre point. This will help keep the work
at the right angle.

On completing this pattern you will have mas-
tered the techniques of simpler Bedfordshire floral designs in preparation for the more intricate
leaf designs and flower motifs to follow.

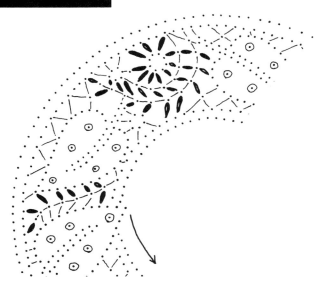

86

Pattern 16

Bookmark sampler of veined leaves

Patterns 13 to 15 dealt with techniques for basic leaves with a central vein. This pattern has been devised as a sampler of both simple leaves and the more intricate ones with side veins. Each of the four main leaves is worked differently.

Introducing The boxed pin-hole, forming side veins by working boxed pin-holes in a continuous line, the gimped side vein.

Materials About 40 pairs of bobbins; 3 pairs for the gimps: Madeira Tanne 50; Coton à Broder No 18 for the gimps.

Techniques

The boxed pin-hole, Fig 16a Boxed pin-holes are used to vary the texture of an area of clothwork. They produce a light definition for side veins in leaves or flower petals. As the diagram shows, all the four pairs surrounding the pin-hole are twisted twice, but this can vary according to the definition required and the thickness of the thread.

On the row immediately above the pin-hole work across the passives to the vein pin-hole, twist the workers and the last passive pair twice; place the pin to mark the position, work a cloth stitch with the next passive pair and twist that pair twice. On the return row twist only the workers twice, underneath the pin. Remove the pin and mark the next boxed pin-hole.

Boxed pin-holes can be worked on a horizontal, vertical or diagonal line. The following patterns illustrate the different uses of this stitch.

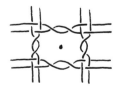

Fig 16a   *Boxed pin-hole*

The two threads on each side are twisted twice.

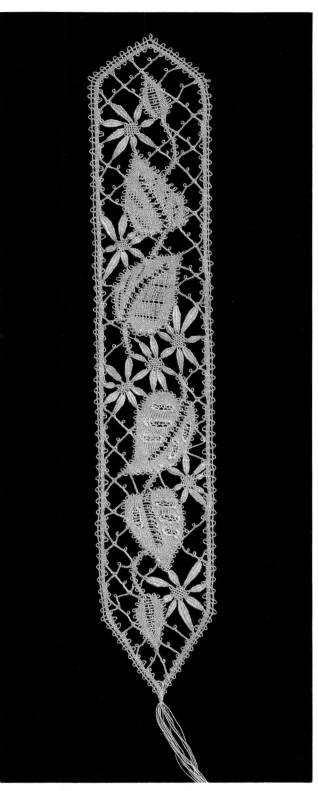

Pl 16

Working the bookmark

Follow Figs 16b to 16h and refer back to Patterns 13 & 14 for the detailed leaf techniques. The top and bottom leaves *1* & *6* are of the simple type with a single vertical vein. The workers meet at the vein pin-hole with either a joining stitch or a kiss stitch. Each of the four main leaves (2 to 5) is worked differently.

Leaves *2* & *3* have side veins formed by boxed pin-holes. In Leaf *2* they are worked on a diagonal line, while in Leaf *3* they are worked on a horizontal or vertical line. The main veins are formed on a row of double pin-holes, as in Leaf 2 of Pattern 14, by a transfer of passives from one half of the leaf to the other.

Different uses of the gimp are shown in Leaves *4* & *5*; both have gimped side veins. Leaf *4* is worked in two halves and Leaf *5* is worked in one; its main vein is formed by one row of gimped pin-holes. The gimp was introduced in Pattern 14 (Leaves *4* & *5*).

Gimped side veins are most often found in the very early examples of these leaves. Strictly speaking, they can be worked only in the horizontal or vertical position within the clothwork. When they are not quite at this angle, the angle of the clothwork working row *may be tilted slightly* away from the usual 90° to the footside.

Setting in, Fig 16b To start working in both directions hang 2 pairs, straddled, at pin-hole *A*. Twist the pairs four times, place the pin, work a cloth stitch with them, and twist each pair once (this is a *false picot*). With these pairs work the twisted edge on either side of the bookmark; remember to twist them once, before and after each edge stitch, as shown in Fig 16b.

Hang in 6 pairs, laying them from side to side of the pillow, for the edge passives, and 2 pairs at pin-hole *B* as the workers; work in both directions. Note the number of twists marked in Fig 16b. Add 2 pairs as marked for the plaits to work the plaited ground with picots.

Leaf 1 Begin the small Leaf *1* with a windmill crossing, then add the single pairs as shown in Fig 16c.

Make the vein with the two pairs of workers, either by crossing them with a kiss stitch or by joining them at the central pin-hole, as follows. Twist the workers twice, work a cloth stitch, twist once, place the pin, work another cloth stitch, and twist twice more.

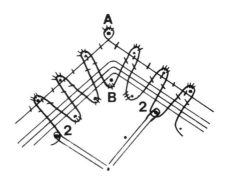

Fig 16b   *Setting in with a false picot at A* (prs)

Take in and leave out pairs for the ground of plaits with picots, and the flower of tallies. At the base of the leaf lay back pairs, so that only four pairs remain for the stalk, plus two pairs needed for a plait leaving the stalk to the right.

Work the flower of tallies and half-stitch bud as shown in Pattern 8.

Leaf 2, Fig 16c & 16d Work the upper part in one up to the top vein pin-hole, adding pairs at the edges as shown. Change the central passive pair into a worker as in Fig 12b (for dividing trails) and work the two halves separately. Leave out a pair at each vein pin-hole on the right-hand side, twisting them twice in readiness for being taken into the left-hand side (see Pattern 14, Leaf 2, Fig 14j).

Follow Fig 16d to make the slanted side veins at the positions marked on the pricking. Start at the top, about 2 pairs in from the right-hand edge, and work in the direction of the arrows. Make 2 to 4 boxed pin-holes, to suit position and preference. Place the pin only to mark the position of the 'box' being worked, and remove it directly the boxed pin-hole is complete; place the pin into the next pin-hole. Remove the pins and allow the threads to fall into place naturally.

To work the side veins on the left-hand side of the leaf follow the arrows in Fig 16d in reverse order.

As the leaf narrows towards the base you need to lay pairs back. At the base itself further pairs will need removing (see Fig 14q, Leaf 5 in Pattern 14); follow the row markings in Fig 16c as a guide. Two pairs should remain at each side of the leaf to make the stalk.

Fig 16c   *Leaves 1 & 2 working diagram* (prs)

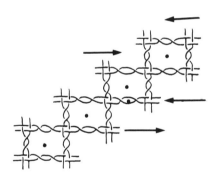

Fig 16d   *Boxed pin-holes on a diagonal line*

The pin-holes are worked one at a time on
following rows.

Pl 16a   *Enlarged top leaves from Pl 16*

Side veins worked using boxed pin-holes.

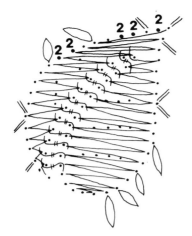

Fig 16e   *Leaf 3 working diagram* (prs)

Leaf 3, Fig 16e-16g   Leaf 3 is also worked in two separate parts, starting from the top vein pin-hole. Work the left-hand side first and leave out pairs at the main vein pin-holes to be later taken into the right-hand half of the leaf. Follow the row markings and number of pairs to be added shown in the diagram.

To work the vertical side veins in the left half follow Fig 16f, and Fig 16g for the horizontal side veins in the right half. The pin-holes of these veins are marked to show their positions. There is no need to *place* the pins; a more natural appearance will be obtained by simply working the boxed pin-holes. You can also experiment with the number of twists to achieve the desired effect. The point is that twisting the pairs not only produces a hole where you want it (round the pin-hole), but also on the other side of the twist (where you don't want it). These are called 'shadow-holes', and the fewer the twists, the smaller the shadow-holes!

Work the spray of flowers across the middle with the pairs left out from Leaf 3 and from the plaits.

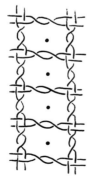

Fig 16f   *Vertical boxed pin-holes*

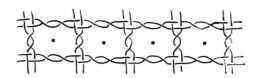

Fig 16g   *Horizontal boxed pin-holes*

Leaf 4, Fig 16h   This third large leaf is also worked in two separate halves, left side first. Note the number of pairs needed to set in the shallow curve. The row markings show that the top left-hand side of the leaf must be formed *before* the stalk is joined into it. Take half the stalk pairs (2) into the left-hand side of the leaf and the other half into the right-hand side.

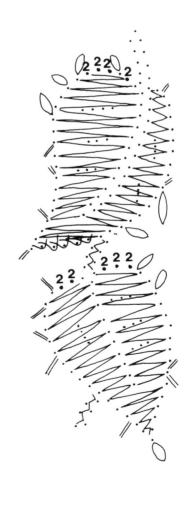

Fig 16h   *Leaves 4 & 5 working diagram* (prs)

90

As you work down the left half, leave out pairs at the vein pin-holes to be taken later into the right-hand side to work the main vein. Work the side veins with gimps as in Leaves *4 & 5* of Pattern 14 (Figs 14m & 14p). They are in a horizontal position on the left half of the leaf, and vertical on the right. For these side veins you must leave the pins in, not remove them as in Leaves *2 & 3* above.

To remove pairs and accommodate the shallow curve at the bottom of the leaf, change passives into workers and then remove them from the clothwork, as for Leaf 5 in Pattern 14, (Fig 14q).

Leaf 5, Fig 16h Both halves of this leaf are worked at the same time with separate workers, pairs being added as marked. Lay a gimp round the main vein and join the workers at the centre pin-hole, as for the vertical vein with gimp in Leaf *4* of Pattern 14, (Fig 14n).

As you can see, the side veins in this leaf are not strictly horizontal nor vertical in relation to the normal angle of the clothwork, so you need to work the clothwork tilted slightly anti-clockwise. Although the clothwork will not be quite at 90° to the footside, it will allow you to work the left side-vein with a gimp on a vertical line. Equally you will be able to work the three side veins with a gimp in the right half as truly horizontal veins.

This is the only exception to the rule, *work at 90° to the footside*.

Work the last, small leaf to match the first one.

Finishing   To finish, join the workers of the edge trail as shown in Fig 12c for Pattern 12. Lay back some pairs from the trail, but leave enough for a tassel.

Pattern 17
Four flower medallions

There are many wonderful designs for flowers in Bedfordshire lace, both naturalistic and stylised. In this section two basic flower shapes will be taught, each with 5 or 6 petals. Each flower, which is worked as a medallion, is placed in two different positions, so it will need to be worked differently in each case.

The boxed pin-holes in the petals provide a little extra texture.

The design for the basic flower motif is derived from the Bedfordshire circle, so working it follows the method of dividing and rejoining clothwork areas described in Pattern 12. This technique is vitally important for Bedfordshire floral lace, and this further exercise will build on what you have learnt already.

Flower motifs are versatile; they can be used for brooches, earrings, dress decoration, and for other accessories such as paperweights.

Introducing Working a Bedfordshire flower from a circle, avoiding 'upwards' working at the inner circle.

Materials About 36 pairs of bobbins: Madeira Tanne 50.

Techniques

Working a flower from a circle, Figs 17a to 17e
As with circles, the main technique in working a flower is the dividing and rejoining of cloth-work areas round an inner circle (see Pattern 12, Fig 12a).

Although the two flower motifs could appear in a variety of positions besides the two shown, the clothwork will *always* divide as at pin-hole x and rejoin at pin-hole y, regardless of position or number of petals.

Figs 17a to 17c show how the basic design for the flower has evolved from the circle. The working lines are the same in each case, and the method of working will also be the same, except that for the flower you must stay within the borders of the individual petals.

Figure 17a is a reminder of how a circle is formed. Starting at pin-hole a, the worker pair works in cloth stitch across the passives, taking in and leaving out pairs as required by the circular shape.

At x you work a cloth stitch with the worker pair and the central passive pair; twist once, place the pin, work another cloth stitch, and twist once more. These two pairs are now worker pairs, each working its own side until level with pin-hole y.

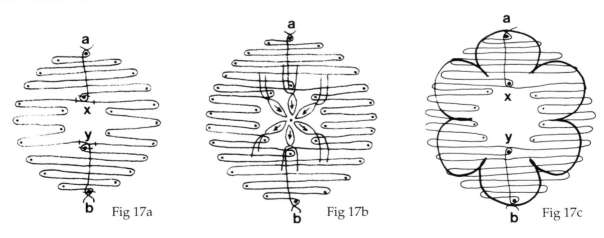

Fig 17a-17c   *The Bedfordshire circle and flower*

The circle, with or without crossed tallies, is worked by dividing and re-joining areas of clothwork at pins x and y. The superimposed flower shape shows its relation to the circle. The working lines are in the same position in both shapes. The areas of clothwork both start at a, divide at x, re-join at y and finish at b. (prs)

92

The two worker pairs join here; twist them once, work a cloth stitch, twist once more, place the pin, and work another cloth stitch. One of the pairs becomes a passive while the other continues as the worker pair to *b*. Work it in cloth stitch across the passives, leaving out or taking in pairs as required by the pattern.

Figure 17b shows how pairs can be left out for a motif in the inner circle and then taken in again.

Figure 17c shows the relation of a flower shape to the circle. The top three petals are set in and worked separately up to a certain level. Two of the worker pairs will meet at a joint pin-hole at the edge of two petals; one of them will become a passive pair while the other works across the central petal and joins the worker pair of the second side petal. One of the worker pairs will continue to the edge of the side petal and work across all three petals, until the clothwork divides, as at pin-hole *x* of a circle. Although this is a summary of the process given in general terms a near example can be seen in Flower 4.

Figure 17d shows how to work the dividing point on the upper part of a shallower inner circle, and a way to avoid working 'upwards' where there are too many rows.

Working upwards would arise if, after dividing the clothwork at pin-hole *x*, the workers were brought back to the next pin-holes, x_1 & x_2. The passives would tend to pull to the sides, creating holes. To avoid this, lay the workers back after pin-hole *x*, as shown, or turn them into passives at a convenient position. Twist the next passive pair on either side of *x* several times and use them as workers to continue the pattern. This will ensure a better outline for the clothwork, as for Leaf 3 of Pattern 14.

Figure 17e shows the lower part of a shallow circle where there are too few rows and the problem shown in Fig 17d can appear in reverse. Here the worker pairs need to re-join at pin-hole *y* before sufficient rows and pin-holes can be worked to produce a satisfactory outline. Twist both worker pairs several times and drop them over pins y_1 & y_2, where they will become passive pairs. Bring the inner edge passive pairs from either side and work the join at pin-hole *y*, as shown.

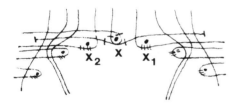

Fig 17d *Dividing the clothwork on a wider curve*

Passive pairs are brought down to work pin-holes x_1 & x_2 when the workers haven't room to do so. (prs)

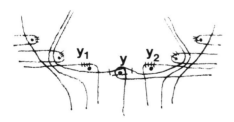

Fig 17e *Re-joining the clothwork on a wider curve*

The first passive pairs from either side of pin *y* are used to work the join when there are too few rows to outline the shallow curve, and the worker pairs are left at pins y_1 & y_2 to become passives. (prs)

Pl 17, *Flower 1*

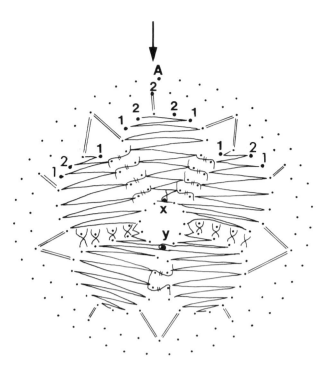

Fig 17f   *Flower 1 working diagram* (prs)

Working the flowers

Flower 1 Five-petalled flower with a central petal at the top, Fig 17f Set in the circular edge as for leaves, adding pairs to make the plaits, as shown.

Set in the top petal. Note the number of pairs to be hung in and follow the working lines. As the shape narrows, leave out single pairs to feed into the side petals. Try to work the boxed pin-holes in the petals without leaving in the pins; it will make the texture a little more flexible. Divide the clothwork area at pin-hole *x* as explained for Fig 17a to 17d above. The flower has an open centre.

Work the two side petals, adding pairs and taking in pairs left out from the top petal. Make a row of upright kiss stitches between these petals and the two bottom ones, as in Leaf 3, Pattern 14, Fig 14l.

You need to start the two bottom petals above the joining pin-hole *y*. First work each petal separately for 2 or 3 rows; then re-join the worker pairs at *y* followed by one row across both petals. Continue working the petals separately, though you need to work a join between them to match the rest of the flower. Work two kiss stitches; alternatively, leave out a single pair from one side, twist twice and take it into the other petal at the same level, as shown: after two rows repeat the process and take it back again.

Leave out pairs as the petals narrow and work plaits to the edge trail.

Complete the pattern as directed for the leaf medallions (Pattern 14, Figs 14g & 14h).

Pl 17a   *Flower 1*

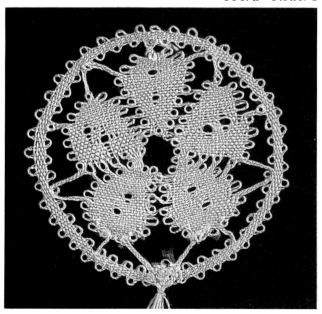

94

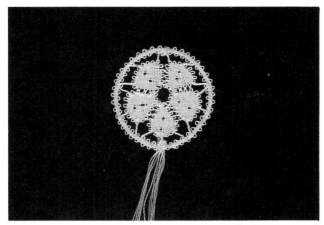

Pl 17, *Flower 2*

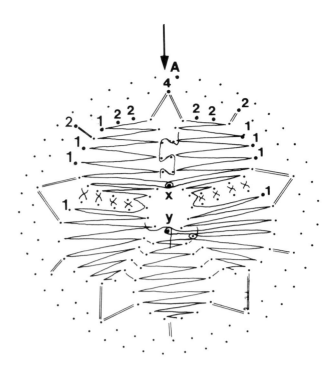

Fig 17g   *Flower 2 working diagram* (prs)

Flower 2 Five petalled flower with two petals at the top, Fig 17g This is another example of a flower motif, with the five petals laid out in reverse order from Flower 1. The exercise shows how a flower needs to be tackled according to the position of its petals in the pattern.

The single boxed pin-holes are intended as a decoration and to vary the texture.

Set in the trail edge as in the previous flower. Work the two top petals simultaneously, adding pairs as indicated. Connect the petals either with kiss stitches or with a twisted pair taken from one to the other and back again, as in Flower 1.

Note the numbers of pairs to be added, shown at the edges of the first two petals. Follow the row markings carefully, especially at the lower ends of these first two petals, where a few more rows need to be worked at the inner circle, to ensure the correct curve.

Work the join to the two side petals with upright kiss stitches, as in Leaf 3, Pattern 14, Fig 14l. Work the side petals, following the row markings. At pin-hole *y* join the passive pair from the left (used as a worker) and the worker from the right.

Work the join between the side petals and the single bottom petal by leaving out pairs at the inner edge pin-holes. Lay back pairs from the outer edge of the side petals, near their base. Watch the direction of the passive pairs carefully so that they continue straight down the pillow without veering to one side or the other. Lay back pairs as soon as there is a sign of crowding.

Finish as for Flower 1.

Pl 17b   *Flower 2*

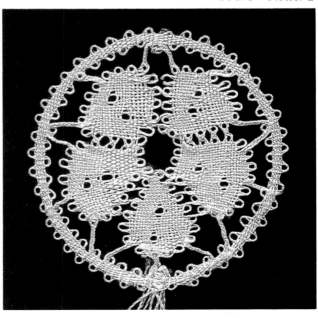

95

Pl 17, *Flower 3*

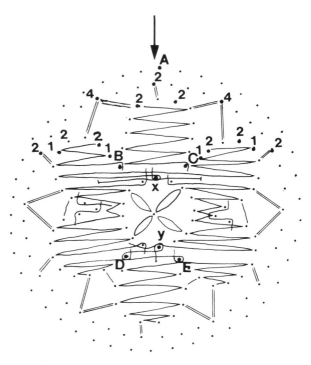

Fig 17h   *Flower 3 working diagram* (prs)

Flower 3 Six petalled flower with a crossing of tallies, Fig 17h This is less common than the five-petalled motif and is found in earlier patterns. The clothwork can be varied or made lighter by boxed pin-holes, veins or raised tallies; all equally effective and open to your choice.

Set in the edge trail as for previous medallions. Work the plaits to the top petal and start it in the same way as for Flower 1.

Start the two adjoining side petals before you have completed the top one, to allow for the join at pin-holes *B* & *C*. Two of the workers become passives, while the worker from the right-hand petal works one or two rows across all three petals. Divide the clothwork at pin-hole *x*.

The inner circle is wider than in the other flowers, so Fig 17d should be followed carefully. Leave out two sets of two pairs for the central crossing of tallies, as shown.

Work the join between the top and the lower side petals by laying back pairs, by carrying pairs through to the lower side-petals and by working a plait, as marked. More than one plait on each side, however, would spoil the outline of the petals.

Follow the row markings closely to keep them level, as it is easy to lose the angle of 90° to the footside. Remember also to take in the tally pairs at the inner circle edge, as shown in Fig 17e.

The tally pairs will be needed to fill odd gaps in the clothwork when the circle is joined at pin-hole *y*. Work one or two rows across the whole width if possible, then divide the clothwork at pin-holes *D* & *E* to complete the three lower petals separately.

The connecting plaits shown, while saving effort, make the petal less well defined. To avoid this you will need to remove the plait pairs and hang in new ones for the bottom petal.

Finish the pattern as for the previous ones.

Pl 17, *Flower 4*

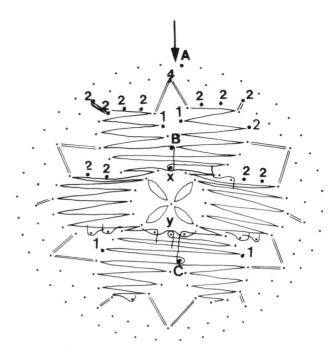

Fig 17i   *Flower 4 working diagram* (prs)

Flower 4 Six petalled flower with different lay-out of petals, Fig 17i   Here is another six-petalled flower to practice a different position of petals in the lace. As the method of working is determined by the position of the petals, working this flower is quite straightforward. The veins are defined by boxed pin-holes.

Set in the circular edge trail as for other medal-lions. Work the two petals separately as far as the joint pin-hole *B*, adding pairs as shown. Work the petals together up to pin-hole *x* where the circle divides.

Follow Fig 17i: you need to add 2 sets of 2 pairs before working the first row of the side petals. At the base of the petals lay the pairs back as shown by the working lines on the diagram.

To join the circle at pin-hole *y* follow Fig 17e closely. Note the change of worker pairs into pas-sives before pin-hole *y* (Fig 17i). After the join work both of the lower petals together until they divide at pin-hole *C*, adding one pair at the edge of each petal as marked. Complete each petal sep-arately. With the remaining pairs work plaits and join them into the edge trail.

Finish the pattern as for the previous ones.

Pl 17d   *Flower 4*

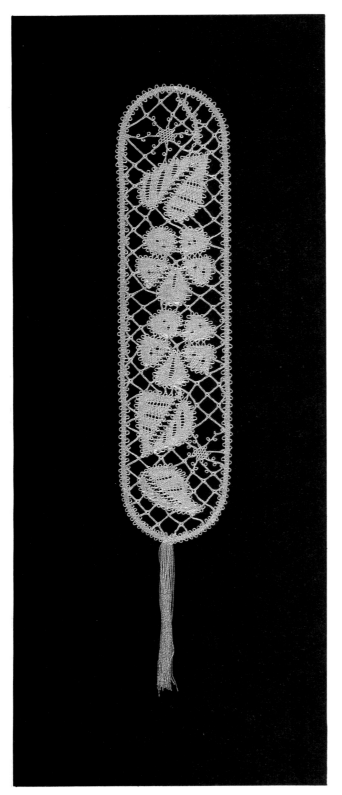

Pattern 18
Floral spray insertion

This pattern provides a practice piece to consolidate the knowledge of flower and leaf techniques already worked; no new techniques are included. It can be used as a small test piece, and perhaps for a little improvisation: only general hints and a working diagram are provided.

Materials About 40 pairs of bobbins: Madeira Tanne 50.

Working the lace

Follow Fig 18a. The pattern contains the five petalled Flower 2 from Pattern 17, and leaves with main and side veins. The lower petals of the flowers have been elongated slightly, and a vein added to emphasise their length and suggest a violet. A gimp can be added round the vein of this petal for even greater emphasis, and as a further exercise in working gimps. The centre of the flower is worked with crossed plaits.

Note the nearly vertical and nearly horizontal side veins in the leaves. They are worked similarly to those in Leaf 3 of Pattern 16. On the pricking their position is marked by lines rather than pin-holes, since even in Leaf 3 (Pattern 16) the pin-holes were used only as a marker; so you will no longer need them for this type of vein.

The purpose of this and the two following patterns is to encourage you to work with a minimum of guidance, and in doing so to become ready to tackle advanced Bedfordshire lace on your own.

Pl 18

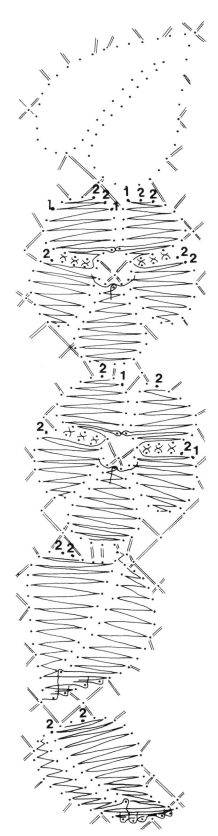

Fig 18a   *Working diagram* (prs)

Leaf shapes are slightly different from earlier patterns. Side veins were worked with horizontal and vertical boxed pin-holes.

Pl 19

Pattern 19
Bookmark with 'blackberries'

Although this pattern resembles the previous one it has other purposes. Three remaining basic techniques are explained: raised and rolled tallies, flat overlaid pointed tallies and the eight-pair crossing. It provides a practice piece for a five petalled flower (Flower 1 from Pattern 17), and for leaves with main veins and horizontal and vertical side veins. Together with the previous pattern and the next, it offers a review of the techniques learned so far and a further stage in working independently.

Introducing The raised and rolled tally, the flat overlaid tally, the eight-pair crossing.

Materials About 50 pairs of bobbins: Madeira Tanne 50.

Techniques

The raised and rolled tally, Fig 19a Work the half-stitch or cloth work area down to the level of the pin-hole. Leave the worker pair aside and carefully pull the passives straight into place; place the pin. With the pairs on either side of the pin work a square-ended tally as explained in Pattern 14, Fig 14a. Make it *twice* as long as it is wide. Lay a support pin *over* the two pairs and wind the pairs over and *under* the support pin, as shown.

Remove the pin from behind the tally. Gently allow the tally to roll back over itself and replace the pin into the same pin-hole, *in front* of the tally. Prop up the support pin behind convenient side pins (Fig 14b). You can remove the support pin after several rows. This makes for a neat, tightly rolled tally, as opposed to the ordinary raised tally which is simply pushed together from the front. The raised and rolled tally was chosen for the 'blackberry' motif since it is less likely to be pulled out of shape by subsequent rows of tallies.

The flat overlaid pointed tally, Fig 19b Flat overlaid tallies are made in the same way as raised tallies, except that their ends are shaped into a point. Two pin-holes within an area of clothwork mark an overlaid tally.

Pull the passive pairs into position when the work is level with the first pin-hole. Place the pin.

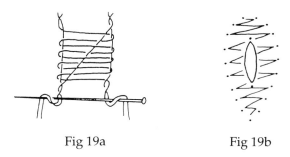

Fig 19a   Fig 19b

Fig 19a   *Raised and rolled tally*

Shows threads round the support pin before the tally is rolled back.

Fig 19b   *Overlaid tally* (prs)

Work the tally with the pairs on either side of the pin. When it is long enough to reach the second pin-hole, lay it out of the way to the back of the pillow. Work the clothwork underneath it until it is level with the second pin-hole. Lay the tally into position, on top of the clothwork. Place the second pin between the two tally pairs after arranging the clothwork passives evenly across the work. Incorporate the tally pairs into the clothwork by working one row across the background.

The eight-pair crossing, Fig 19c   In an eight-pair crossing, four plaits or tallies meet at a pin-hole, cross each other, and continue. The arrows show where the pairs come from, and that they continue in the same direction after the crossing.

Use each pair as one thread and work as follows.

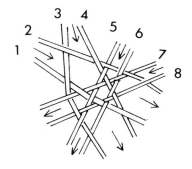

Fig 19c   *Eight-pair crossing*

Follow the numbers and arrows for the order of working.

Pl 19a   *Enlarged 'blackberries' from Pl 19*

Note the cluster of raised tallies over the half-stitch ground. The gimp enhances the outline of the leaves.

Work a half-stitch with the 4 centre pairs *3, 4, 5 & 6*

Work a half-stitch with the 4 right-hand pairs *5, 6, 7 & 8*

Work a half-stitch with the 4 left-hand pairs *1, 2, 3 & 4*

Repeat with the 4 centre pairs, the 4 right-hand pairs and the 4 left-hand pairs.

Place the pin and work a cloth stitch with the 4 centre pairs *3, 4, 5 & 6*

Cross pair *2* over *3* and *6* over *7*.

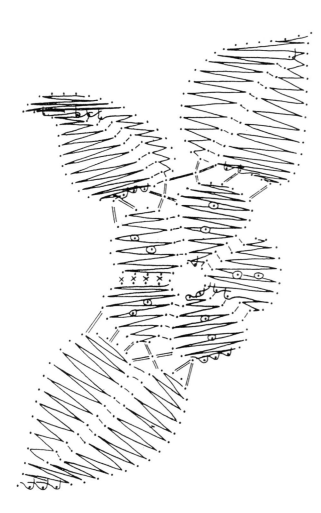

Fig 19d   *Working diagram* (prs)

Working the lace, Fig 19d

Note the 'false picots' at the start of the bookmark (as at pin-hole G in Fig 2h, Pattern 2b). They are not marked on the pricking, but are used to hang in enough pairs for the edge trail *and* the ground. Alternatively you can work an ordinary trail as in Pattern 4 (Figs 4g & 4h), adding the pairs for the ground on the inner side of the trail.

The 'blackberry' shapes can be worked in cloth stitch or half-stitch and the raised texture can be achieved with raised tallies over clothwork or over half-stitch. Alternatively, boxed pin-holes can be worked on a clothwork shape.

If you decide to make the 'blackberry' shapes in half-stitch, near the base you should change to cloth stitch, from which it will be easier to remove pairs. I chose myself to make rolled raised tallies over the half-stitch 'blackberry' shapes. As there are so many over a small space, and because of the way they are made, it is less likely they will be pulled out of shape by the subsequent row of tallies.

Fig 19d is a guide to working the leaf and flower arrangement.

Finishing   Use the techniques explained in Figs 4c & 4d, Pattern 4.

Pl 20

Pattern 20

Bedfordshire flower and leaf medallion

If you have followed through the exercises in this book, you will now be able to work this pattern on your own without detailed instructions, though the diagrams and photographs should help. It will be especially pleasing to those who like using lots of bobbins!

The pattern is an adaptation of motifs from a pricking for a collar in the collection of Abington Park Museum, Northampton. They are arranged within the smallest possible area of lace, while retaining their original sizes.

The challenge of this pattern lies in the treatment of the trails which enclose the leaf shapes.

At the beginning and end they are worked as circles, while in between they are treated as trails. This means that the starting and finishing points fall in awkward positions and require special attention.

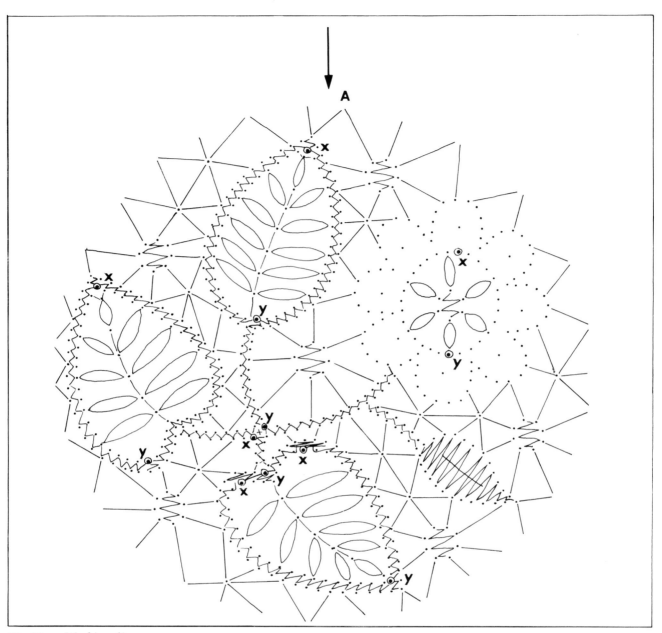

Fig 20a *Working diagram*

The ringed pin-holes indicate where trails divide or re-join. (prs)

Materials About 68 pairs of bobbins: Madeira Tanne 30.

Working the lace

Follow Fig 20a to set in and add pairs, and work down the pattern. I have chosen pin-hole A for the beginning because the flower is then in a position similar to that of Flower 3 in Pattern 17. It is worked in the same way, with the addition of a petal on either side, and a half-stitch bud for the centre. The pin-holes in the centres of the petals were worked as raised tallies: they could also be used to work boxed pin-holes.

The arrows in Fig 20a indicate the direction for working plaits and tallies; and lines show the working rows. The trails enclosing the leaf shapes are worked partly as circles. The points where these circles divide and join are marked by ringed pin-holes. See Pattern 12, Figs 12a-c for these techniques.

Pl 20a   *Enlarged centre of Pl 20*

Shows the crossing of the stalk trails, first worked in Pattern 6, and the
beginning of the bottom leaf which was started separately.

To join the leaf stalks follow the instructions for
crossing of trails in Pattern 6, Fig 6a.

Picots are not marked on the pricking; you
should decide yourself if and where to make
them.

If you wish to work independently you can
chose a different starting point, as long as you

work evenly through, from the top pin-hole on
the circular edge trail to the bottom.

You should now be ready to tackle the fine Bedfordshire floral lace in my first book, *Traditional
Bedfordshire Lace.*

GOOD LUCK!

105

Prickings

Pattern 1

Designed by the author

Pattern 2a & 2b

Adapted by the author from an old patten

Pattern 4

Adapted by the author from an old patten

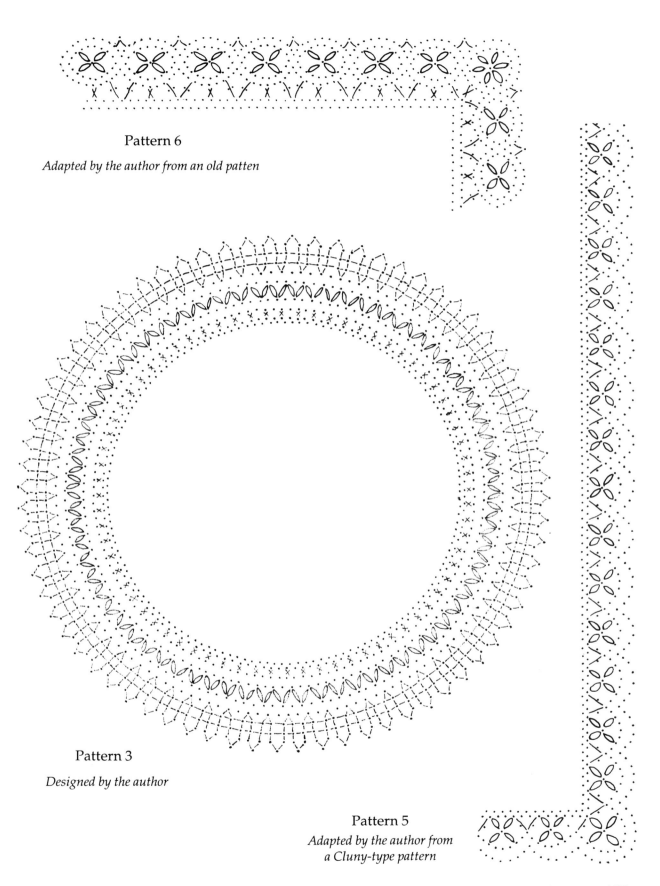

Pattern 6

Adapted by the author from an old patten

Pattern 3

Designed by the author

Pattern 5

*Adapted by the author from
a Cluny-type pattern*

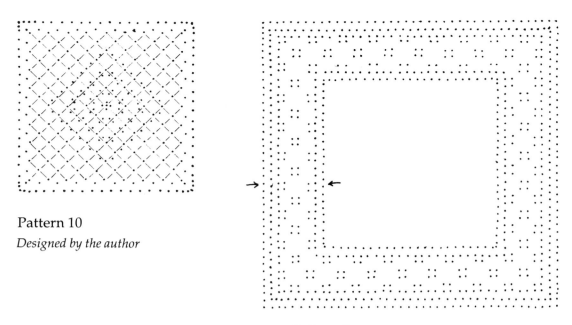

Pattern 10
Designed by the author

Pattern 9
Designed by the author

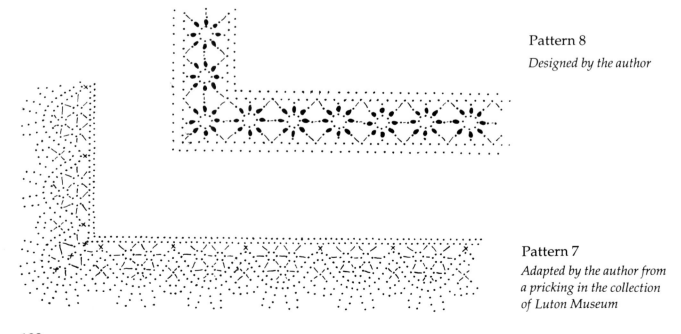

Pattern 8
Designed by the author

Pattern 7
*Adapted by the author from
a pricking in the collection
of Luton Museum*

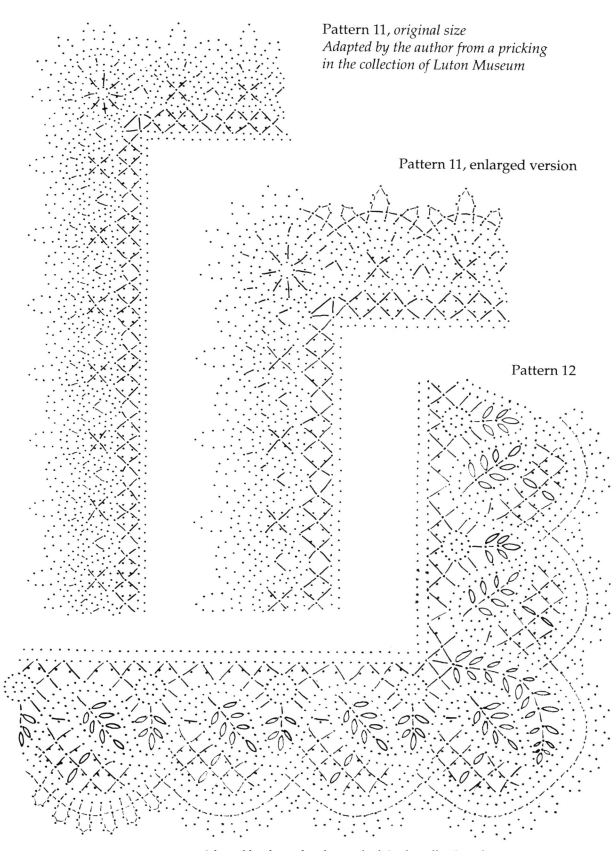

Pattern 11, *original size*
Adapted by the author from a pricking
in the collection of Luton Museum

Pattern 11, enlarged version

Pattern 12

Adapted by the author from a draft in the collection of
Luton Museum

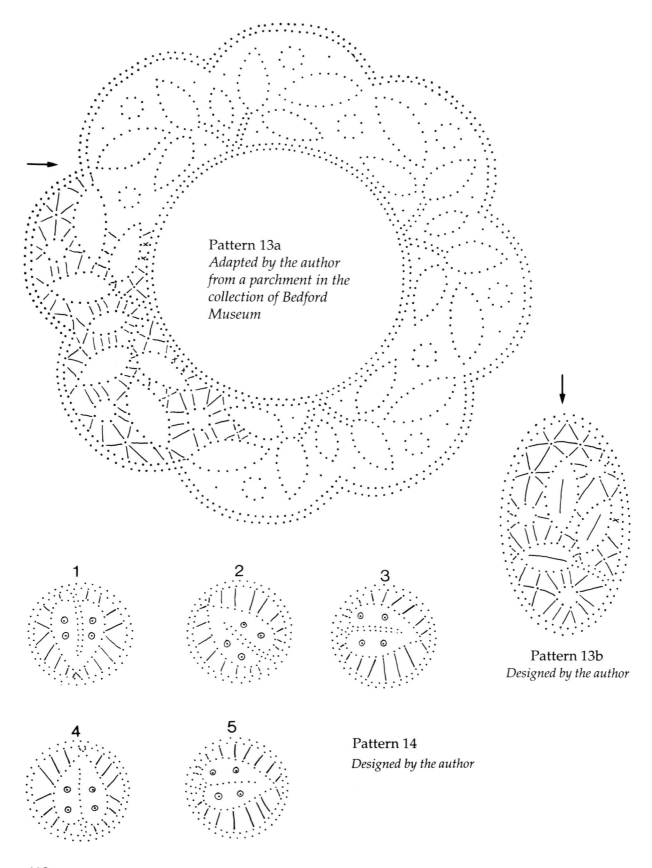

Pattern 13a
*Adapted by the author
from a parchment in the
collection of Bedford
Museum*

Pattern 13b
Designed by the author

1

2

3

4

5

Pattern 14
Designed by the author

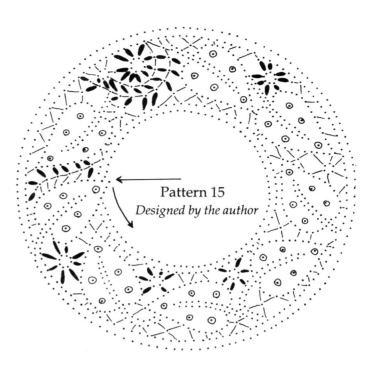

Pattern 15
Designed by the author

Pattern 17 *Designed by the author*

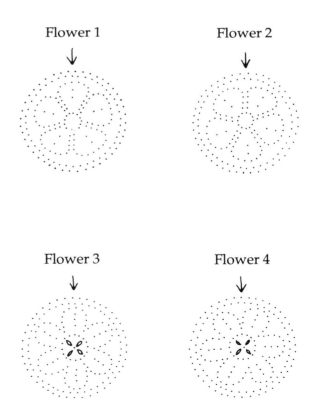

Flower 1

↓

Flower 2

↓

Flower 3

↓

Flower 4

↓

Pattern 16
Designed by the author

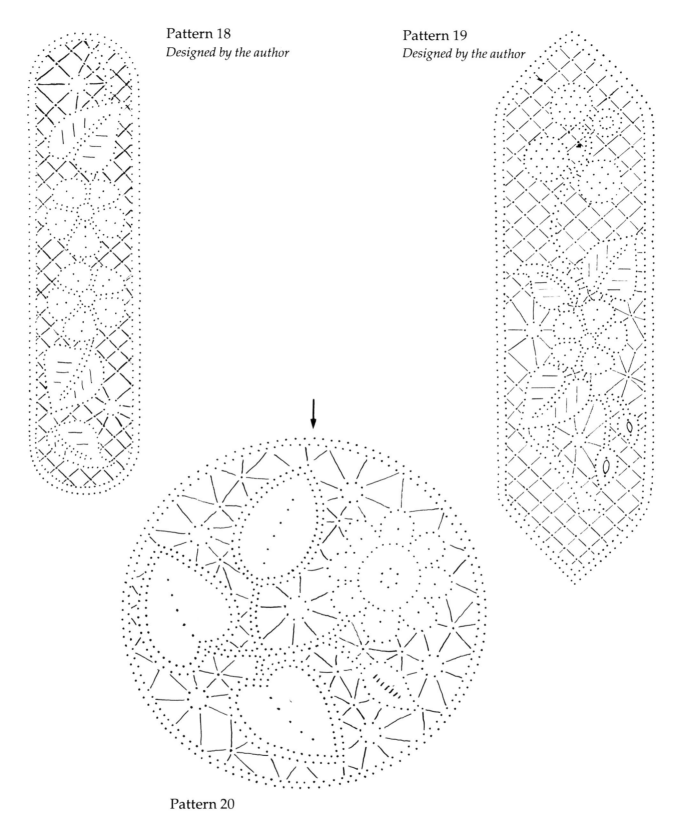

Pattern 18
Designed by the author

Pattern 19
Designed by the author

Pattern 20

Adapted from a parchment for a collar in the collection of
Abington Park Museum, Northampton

Additional prickings

Handkerchief border and corner, see centre spread
Adapted from a draft in the collection of the Cecil
Higgins Art Gallery, Bedford

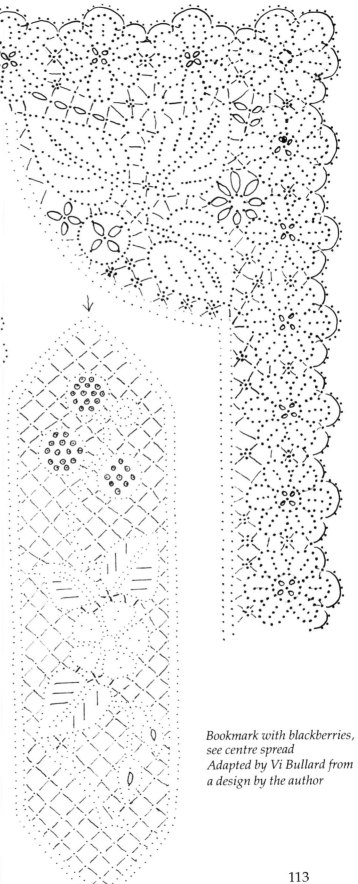

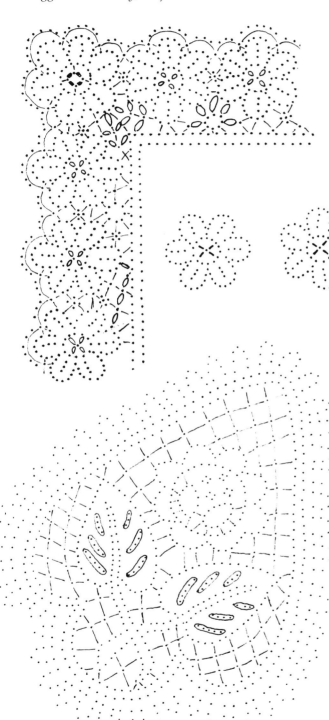

Bonnet back, see centre spread

Bookmark with blackberries,
see centre spread
Adapted by Vi Bullard from
a design by the author

113

Glossary

Bar — see Plait.

Barleycorn — old Bedfordshire term for a square-ended tally (see below).

Bedfordshire ground — Ground means the area of lace between the headside with its motifs and the footside (see below). The term originally denoted the undecorated mesh of all East Midlands lace and continues to be used for Bucks point ground. With the introduction of the Maltese type lace and fillings from Honiton lace Bedfordshire ground was increasingly worked with plaits and tallies.

It also combines with several motifs to form the Blossom ground (Pattern 10), Flower ground (Pattern 8), Plaited ground (Pattern 9) and Spider ground (Pattern 7).

Boxed pin-hole — method of outlining a vein on a leaf or petal motif.

Bud — a rounded unit of design in Bedfordshire lace worked in half-stitch (Pattern 4).

Circle — area of clothwork (worked in cloth stitch) that divides and re-joins to form a circular shape (Pattern 12). It is the basis of the flower motifs in Bedfordshire Floral lace (Pattern 17, Flowers 1-4).

Close or enclose — the working of the second half of a stitch after the pin has been placed.

Cloth stitch — one of the two basic stitches used in Bedfordshire lace, worked with 2 pairs of bobbins (see The stitches, Diags C & D).

Clothwork (toile) — area of lace worked in cloth stitch giving the effect of woven fabric.

Cross — to place a left-hand thread (or pair) over a right-hand one (see The stitches, Diag A).

Crossings — where plaits and trails meet, cross each other and continue in the same direction.

Windmill, a crossing of four plaits (Pattern 1); *six-pair* crossing (Pattern 2); *eight-pair* crossing (Pattern 19).

Trail pairs of different widths cross at different angles (Pattern 6).

Dividing a trail — parting a trail and working the parts separately (Pattern 12).

False picot — a method of adding pairs (Patterns 2 & 16).

Filling — term derived from Honiton lace where it denotes stitches used to fill areas within motifs, e.g. Blossom filling. Sometimes used in Bedfordshire for ground (see *Bedfordshire ground* above).

Footside — the straight edge of the lace, where it can be joined to other material. In English laces the footside is worked on the right-hand side (see Equipment and basic techniques, Diag I).

Gimp — a thick, soft thread which serves to outline parts of the design (Patterns 14, 16 & 17).

Ground — see *Bedfordshire ground* above.

Half-stitch — the second basic stitch for Bedfordshire lace, in which only one thread of the worker pair traverses the passive threads, giving the lace a more open appearance (see Equipment and basic techniques, Diags E & F).

Half-stitch and twist — stitch worked like a cloth stitch with an added twist (see Equipment and basic techniques, Diags *G & H*).

Hanging in — placing a pair or pairs of bobbins round a pin to start work (see also *Setting in* below).

Head — one repeat of the design.

Headside — outer edge of the lace, mostly scalloped and decorated. In English lace the headside is worked on the left-hand side.

Kiss stitch — a method of connecting two parts of a pattern, by exchanging worker pairs (Pattern 3).

Laying back pairs — discarding unwanted threads by laying them to the back of the pillow, to be cut off when the pins are removed (Figs 7b & 7c).

Leaving out pairs — setting pairs aside to work another section of the pattern later.

Leg — see *Plait* below.

Lifting the lace — see Setting up in Pattern 1.

Marker pin — pin (and pin-hole) used only to indicate where a stitch is to be worked. The pin does not remain in the lace (see *kiss stitch*, Pattern 3).

Ninepin edge — an arrangement of plaits forming an outer edge characteristic of Bedfordshire lace from the mid-19th century onwards (Pattern 1).

Overlaid flat tallies — see *Tally* below.

Passives (passive pairs) — the threads hanging down on the pillow which the workers work through. In weaving terms the passives would be the warp.

Picots (headpins) — decorative loops made on the headside of the lace or on plaits (Patterns 1 & 2).

Plait (*bride*, leg or bar) — a continuous half-stitch braid worked with four threads. In parts of Bedfordshire this term is also interchangeable with tallies, wheatears and barleycorns. Plaits are used to fill areas within, and between, parts of the design. They can be decorated with picots (see *above*).

Pointed tally — see *Tally* below.

Removing pairs — discarding surplus pairs. Several methods are given (e.g. Patterns 2, 4, 5, 7, 10).

Re-pinning — using a pin-hole twice, notably at a corner to obtain a neater angle (Pattern 5, Fig 5f).

Setting in — hanging pairs over a pin, or pins, to start work (Pattern 1).

Setting up — moving a length of worked lace back to the beginning of the pricking (Pattern 1).

Stitches — units of working the lace; see *Cloth stitch, Half-stitch, Half-stitch and twist* above; also Equipment and basic techniques.

Sewing — term from other lace-making techniques for a join made with looped threads. Not used in traditional Bedfordshire lace, except to join two ends of a finished border (Pattern 1).

Taking in pairs — incorporating pairs into a section of lace.

Tally — small solid decoration made with four threads, one thread weaving over and under the other three. It can be pointed (Pattern 2), square-ended (Pattern 9), overlaid flat, or rolled (Pattern 19).

Temporary pin — a pin placed outside the pattern to anchor a new pair or pairs while being incorporated into the lace (Pattern 1, Figs 1a & 1f).

Trail — a curving, continuous band of clothwork, forming headside edge scallops and other features of the design, introduced into Bedfordshire lace from Maltese lace in the mid-19th century.

Twist — to place a right-hand thread (or pair) over the left-hand one (see Equipment and Basic techniques, Diag *B*).

Twisted edge pair — see *Winkie pin* below.

Windmill — a crossing of four plaits (legs); see also *Crossings* above.

Winkie pin — loop formed by twisting the worker pair round the edge pin (Pattern 3).

Workers (worker pair) — a pair of threads which work through the passive pairs. In weaving terms they would be the weft.

Working row — horizontal line on which the worker pair proceeds from one passive pair to another, across an area of clothwork; normally worked at a 90° angle to the footside.

Other Lace, Costume and Embroidery Books available from Ruth Bean

In the Cause of English Lace Catherine Channer/Anne Buck
0 903585 26 X   218mm X 160mm, 112p 32ill, hardbound

Miss Channer's Lace Mat: Full size pattern supplement to above book
Folded illustrated sheet 532 X 393mm + pricking on card 393 X 266mm

Traditional Bedfordshire Lace Barbara Underwood
0 903585 24 3   270 X 212mm, 100p, 200ill, folding sheet, hardbound

Bedfordshire Lace Patterns – A selection by Margaret Turner
0 903585 21 9   280 X 210mm, 112p, 145ill, folding sheet, limpbound

Manual of Bedfordshire Lace Pamela Robinson
0 903585 20 0   247 X 233mm, 112p, 151ill, limpbound

Lace Flowers and How to Make Them Joyce Willmot
0 903585 23 5   187 X 156mm, 76p 46pl & diagr incl colour, hardbound

The Technique & Design of Cluny Lace L Paulis/Maria Rutgers
0 903585 18 9   220 X 174mm, 96p, 130ill, hardbound

Victorian Costume & Costume Accessories Anne Buck
0m 903585 17 0   220 X 174mm, 224p, 90ill, paperback

Le Pompe 1559 Santina Levey/Pat Payne
(Patterns for Venetian Bobbin Lace)
0 903585 16 2   243 X 177mm, 128p, 97ill, paperback

Teach Yourself Torchon Lace Eunice Arnold
0 903585 08 1   240 X 190mm, 40p, 6workcards, 27ill, limpbound

Victorian Lace Patricia Wardle
0 903585 13 8   222 X 141mm, 304p, 82pl, hardbound

Thomas Lester His Lace & E Midlands Industry 1820–1905 Anne Buck
0 903585 09 X   280 X 210mm, 120p, 55pl, hardbound

The Needlework of Mary Queen of Scots Margaret Swain
0 903585 22 7   280 X 212, 128p, 89pl incl 12 colour, paperback